BECOMING A BARRISTER:

Getting pupillage

and a career at the Bar

Becoming a Barrister:
Getting pupillage
and a career at the Bar

*The essential guide on what to know, what
to do and how to do it!*

Matthew Thorne

First Edition 2017

ISBN: 1542688612
ISBN-13: 978-1542688611

This book is intended as a guide for use by those considering a career as a barrister at the Bar of England and Wales, those who wish to help them, and those who simply wish to know more. It considers the nuts and bolts of life as a barrister, what you need to be thinking about and doing to maximise your chances, and how to reach the prize of pupillage.

Matthew Thorne is a practising barrister in chambers in London. His work is primarily focussed on commercial, construction and insurance law. Having received a first class degree in Law at the University of Cambridge, and 'Outstanding' on the Bar Professional Training Course, he was called to the Bar by the Honourable Society of the Inner Temple in 2011 and was granted tenancy in 2012.

For my family, to whom I owe my career at the Bar.

Overview

Table of Contents

Chapter 1: Introduction

You will have heard it said that prostitution is the oldest profession. The legal profession is not far behind, and it often appears to the outsider that little has changed over the centuries.[1]

Whilst it is true that it retains many of its historical peculiarities, the Bar of England and Wales has, in fact, evolved into a modern, dynamic and outward-looking environment. It continues to dictate the direction of legal development through the thought, advice and argument of its senior practitioners; yet over recent decades it has also transformed into an open, client-focussed and commercial enterprise.

It is difficult to think of many other professions with the scope, breadth and diversity of work in which, as a barrister, you may find yourself engaged. Even after you have chosen the area in which you will practise (be it in crime, human rights, tax, family, land, shipping, employment, media, construction or one of the many other

---

[1] For a detailed analysis of the English legal historical background, see *An Introduction to English Legal History*, J.H. Baker (4th Ed).

specialist disciplines), you will find that no day is ever the same. It is not unimaginable that you may find yourself crossing swords with a French *avocat* in a multi-lingual arbitration one day, wading through a muddy field on a site visit the next, and finishing off the week in your office in chambers, drafting detailed submissions to the Court of Appeal on the finer intricacies of the latest legislation, before packing your bags in preparation for next week's trip across the country for a morning conference at a client's premises. And even on those weeks which are spent behind your desk in chambers, the chances are you will be working on a number of different cases, each with its own interesting fact pattern, clients and legal problems.

It is also worth making clear at the outset that, contrary to common perception, the Bar is not a closed shop or a profession in which you need 'contacts' to get started. If ever there was, in decades or centuries past, an element of favouritism or nepotism in the selection process, no longer can tenancy at the top chambers be obtained through good connections or family ties.[2] Nothing which is worth having is easy to achieve, and a successful career at the Bar is based firmly on merit. Do not be discouraged by a fear of the unknown, a niggle that you may not fit in, or reservations because your family has no background in law or, perhaps, in higher education at all. If you are capable, work hard and plan ahead, tenancy is yours for the taking.

---

[2] This unfortunately still appears to be a common misconception. In fact, since the nature of the job is sink or swim, recruitment on the basis of merit is vital in order to maintain the quality and reputation of a set.

The flip side to this, however, is that competition for places in barristers' chambers is immense. Applicants can be competing against tens and sometimes hundreds of others for one available pupillage place. Unless you are the best *and* are able to demonstrate on the day of interview that you are the best, your years of training may well be in vain. It is a tough path to tread and many never reach the final goal. If you pursue this career, do so with your eyes wide open, an acceptance of the risk and a dedicated attitude.

There is a strong sense of collegiality amongst members of the Bar. This is particularly so on the circuits,[3] and within the specialist disciplines, where barristers will find themselves appearing alongside or against the same barristers on a regular basis, and at the same attending social and professional engagements. It is not unusual, for example, to have a fierce battle in court and then to leave for a committee on which you both sit, or for a dinner at which you will both be present.

Despite its meritocratic underpinnings, the Bar retains a certain mystique found in few professions. Whilst there has been an effort in recent years to 'open up' the Bar and increase awareness and access, to the outside world it can still seem opaque; and the high levels of competition for

---

[3] The Bar of England and Wales is divided into 6 regions or 'circuits', known as the 'Midland', 'Northern', 'North Eastern', 'South Eastern', 'Wales and Chester' and 'Western' circuits. Barristers apply to join a circuit, which provide various services to their members (including support, advice, training, social events, representing the circuit on the Bar Council and maintain channels of communication with the rest of the legal profession). For more information and contact details, see http://www.barcouncil.org.uk/about-the-bar/what-is-the-bar/circuits

pupillage and tenancy only serve to increase the sense of exclusivity.

This book seeks to unshroud the mystery. It will follow the typical pathway to a career at the Bar, beginning with questions as to whether the Bar is the right career to take, and ending with what one might expect during pupillage and in life at the Bar. It is intended to shed a little light on parts of the process which are too rarely discussed and to give a barrister's perspective on things to look out for on the path to tenancy.

Chapter 2: Is this the career for me?

If you are coming to this book as a school or undergraduate student, without having had a previous career, the idea of deciding which profession you will pursue may be daunting. That is understandable: it is one of the biggest commitments you will make. Training can be lengthy, costly and difficult. You should put careful thought into the route you are taking. Carry out thorough research, undertake work experience and talk to professionals doing the job.

My own introduction to life at the Bar came through work experience given to me by a barrister practising in criminal work in Leeds, where I grew up.[4] Though I had no real interest in the law at all, pupils at my school were required to arrange work experience and I thought that watching people in wigs would be as good as anything else. I was only meant to be there for five days but, by the end of the week, I found myself well and truly immersed in the trial of six defendants for attempted murder and continued attending Court through my school holidays to watch the rest of the trial. Well over a decade later, I still vividly recall the description of how the defendants had rammed the victim's

[4] See Chapter 8 for information on work experience.

car, shot at him three times, wounded him with a sword and a machete, and then used a stun gun on him. In sentencing four of the men for a combined total of 46 years, the Judge said that, *"This was an act of vengeance. It was a brutal, vicious and pitiless attack in which you showed your victim no mercy."*

What had been intended as a box-ticking exercise to pacify my teachers entirely shaped my education and career going forward. I was a convert to the Bar.

That is, of course, not the way for everyone. Some will have the opposite reaction to their work experience, but that is just as valuable and, until you try, you will not know.

Whilst this book aims to walk you through some of the most common questions and scenarios, there is no substitute for testing it out yourself. All prospective lawyers, whether barristers, solicitors or other legal professionals, should take as much work experience as they can get their hands on.

In the meantime, let us begin by looking at a number of indicators:

1.   Are you interested in the Law?

        (a) Legislation

        (b) The Common Law

2.   What kind of role are you suited to?

        (a) Barristers

(b) Solicitors

(c) Other legal professionals

Interest in the Law

Let's start with the most obvious question. Are you interested in the law?

This question is more difficult to deconstruct than appears at first blush. Not many people spend their evenings absorbed in abstract legal theory and, if such a prospect fails to fill you with overwhelming enthusiasm, don't close this book just yet. You're not alone. It doesn't necessarily mean that you are *not* interested in the law.

Interest in law goes deeper than abstract theory. The legal landscape in England and Wales is a living, breathing and ever-changing creature. The main sources of law are, first, legislation created or authorised by Parliament, and second, the common law, which is a body of law developed by the judiciary incrementally over many generations.[5] There is, in addition, a body of European law largely stemming from European regulations and directives.[6]

Lawyers have a significant impact on both legislation and the common law. Let's take each of these in turn.

---

[5] For a more comprehensive exposition of the constitutional legal framework, see *Constitutional and Administrative Law*, Bradley, Ewing & Knight (16th Ed).

[6] In the light of the 2016 referendum, it remains to be seen for how long and in what way these continue to apply.

<u>Legislation.</u>

Parliament is often said to be 'sovereign'. It is the principal law making body in our country.[7]

Nevertheless, when drafting and enacting statutes, it obviously cannot always predict or make provision for every possible situation which may eventuate. Statutes will set out the basic principles of law, but how those principles apply to different factual scenarios is often left up to the courts.

Example

For example, the Limitation Act 1980 sets out the deadlines or "limitation periods" in which certain types of claim must be brought against a wrongdoer. At the end of the limitation period, time "expires" and it becomes too late to start a claim. The claim is lost.

In a claim for negligence, the limitation period expires 6 years after the date of damage. But Parliament did not set out an exhaustive definition of 'damage' or what awareness was needed of the relevant damage.

---

[7] Certain powers have also been conferred on the United Kingdom devolved assemblies. In addition, in some circumstances, the UK Government has the ability to create 'secondary' legislation in compliance with powers conferred by Parliament.

This gave rise to an interesting problem for the Courts to solve in the case of *Pirelli General Cable Works Ltd v Oscar Faber & Partners.*[8] The Claimants engaged the Defendant engineers to design a chimney at their factory. Work was completed in July 1969, but a material which had been used was unsuitable for its purpose and cracks began to appear at the top of the chimney by April 1970. Because of the location of the cracks, the Claimants did not become aware of them until November 1977. A claim was issued in October 1978. The Defendants argued that the claim was too late, because damage had occurred more than 6 years before the claim was issued. The House of Lords agreed, holding that the "damage" had occurred in April 1970, even though this was more than six years before the Claimants even knew they had a claim!

This meant that the claim automatically failed because it had been made outside the statutory time limits.

Likewise, exactly what a provision *means* should be self-explanatory, but all too often it is not, and queries remain over how the legislation should be interpreted.

---

[8] [1983] 2 AC 1. The case concerned the Limitation Act 1939, which preceded the 1980 Act of the same name.

Example

In the case of *Pinner v Everett* [1969] 1 WLR 1266, the appellant had been driving his Ford Zodiac on the A1 on his way home. His car was followed for about 2 miles by a police patrol car. The officers made no criticism of his driving but noticed that the rear number plate of his car was not illuminated as required by the Vehicles (Excise) Act, 1949. They signalled him to stop, and he did so in a normal way. There was conversation between the appellant and the police officers, in the course of which the police officers noticed that his breath smelled of alcohol. He was required to perform a breath test, which he failed, and was therefore arrested.

The House of Lords (the previous iteration of the Supreme Court) had to consider whether the police were entitled to require a breath test by reason of their suspecting him of having alcohol in his body, even though they had no reason to suspect him of that whilst he had been physically driving.

This hinged upon the interpretation of section 2 (1) of the Road Safety Act, 1967, which authorised a constable to require *"any person driving or attempting to drive a motor vehicle"* to take such a test if the constable *"has reasonable cause — (a) to suspect him of having alcohol in his body. ..."*

The crucial question was whether the appellant was "driving or attempting to drive" when the constable requested him to provide a specimen of his breath. The appellant was certainly in charge of his car at the relevant time but was he then driving or attempting to drive it?

Lord Reid gave the general rule for interpretation as follows: *"In determining the meaning of any word or phrase in a statute the first question to ask always is what is the natural or ordinary meaning of that word of phrase in its context in the statute? It is only when that meaning leads to some result which cannot reasonably be supposed to have been the intention of the legislature, that it is proper to look for some other possible meaning of the word or phrase..."*

He then continued, *"I must therefore consider in what circumstances a person can, by the ordinary usage of the English language, properly be said to be driving a car. Clearly the term cannot be limited to periods during which the car is in motion. Suppose the car is held up in a traffic jam and is stationary for five or ten minutes. No one would say that the driver is not driving the car during that period. He may have switched off the engine and be reading a book or a map; or he may have got out to clean his windscreen; and I do not think that it would make any difference if he got out to buy a paper from a newsvendor on the pavement. But, on the other hand, suppose the driver pulls up at the kerb and leaves his car to go shopping. I do not think that it could be said that he is driving the car while he is buying groceries. And I do not*

> *think that it would make any difference if he remained in the car while his passenger was doing the shopping: he would then not be driving but waiting for his passenger."*

> Having given his interpretation of "driving or attempting to drive", Lord Reid went on to conclude that, *"in the present case it would seem from the findings which I have quoted that an appreciable period of time must have elapsed before the police officers noticed the smell of alcohol, formed their suspicions, and required the breath test to be taken. During that period they were conversing with him about other matters which had nothing to do with his driving — the unilluminated number plates and a routine check on the identity of drivers. So the question is whether at the time when the breath test was required the appellant could still fairly be said to be driving his car. I find this case to be very near the borderline but with some hesitation I am prepared to agree with the majority of your Lordships that the appellant was then no longer driving his car within the ordinary meaning of the words."*

> The appellant's conviction was therefore quashed.

When a court comes to make decisions in cases turning on legislative provisions, the judgment it gives will be based upon the arguments presented to it by the lawyers for the different parties. So, as you will have seen from the above examples, when a Court makes decisions concerning legislation, barristers have a significant impact on what its provisions are found to mean and how they are found to apply to the situation in issue.

The Common Law.

The common law is a very different beast to Parliamentary legislation. It is a body of rules developed by judges over centuries, incrementally expanded to cover the particular issue under consideration on the day.

Historically, the courts would look at a case and, having heard argument from the Bar, 'declare' the legal rules which applied to it.

The judges would not usually go as far as to suggest that they were creating new rules – on the contrary, they are often at pains to make clear that the creation of new rules is the job of Parliament and that they are simply applying established principles. But in reality, creating new rules is precisely what they are doing.

> **Example**
>
> A stark example is in the field of nuisance (a species of tort law[9]). In very simple terms, a nuisance is committed when the owner of Property A uses the land in an unnatural or unreasonable manner and

---

[9] Tort law is a general term encompassing a variety of civil wrongs, the precise contents of which are beyond the scope of this book. For further information, see Tony Weir's *Introduction to Tort Law.*

thereby causes to the owner of Property B a foreseeable interference with the use or enjoyment of Property B.

As you will have noted, nuisance generally requires a degree of unreasonableness or 'fault'.

But in 1866, in a case known as *Rylands v Fletcher*,[10] the Courts brought into being a new, strict liability for those who bring onto and collect on their land anything 'likely to do mischief if it escapes'. If it does escape, they are liable for the natural consequences whether or not they have acted negligently or unreasonably.

So, in that case, the Defendant constructed a reservoir. Unknown to him, the land was above old mine workings which went underground between his land and that of his neighbour. As the reservoir was being filled, it collapsed and caused flooding through the mine shafts and tunnels, going into the claimant's adjoining mines and causing significant damage. The Court held that, notwithstanding the absence of negligence, he was liable for the damage: he had brought onto his land a man-made accumulation of water which was likely to cause damage if it escaped. He was therefore liable for the damage when it did escape, even though he had not acted unreasonably.

---

[10] *Fletcher v Rylands* (1865-66) L.R. 1 Ex. 265. The decision was subsequently affirmed by the House of Lords in 1868: see (1868) L.R. 3 H.L. 330

> Whilst the Court in 1866 did not suggest it was setting out any new rules,[11] the scope and nature of the law of nuisance was in fact fundamentally expanded.
>
> The impact of this case was significant, and its principles are still applied across courts today.

The common law rules have been expanded, detailed and rationalised over time. They have been taken and re-applied to new scenarios and have come to form a coherent body of laws outside the legislation enacted by Parliament. For example, the entire legal framework surrounding contracts – how people enter into them, and what is the meaning, effect or scope of the contract – stems from common law principles developed by the courts over the years.

So, as can be expected, in much the same way as with legislation, lawyers have a significant impact in the development of the common law: What exactly *are* the principles which have been developed? *Do* they apply to the situation under consideration? *How* do they apply? Should the rules be reconsidered and, perhaps, changed? What is the correct legal outcome? These are all questions that lawyers consider and argue on a regular basis, and their impact in the development of the law cannot be underestimated.

---

[11] See Lord Bingham in *Transco Plc v Stockport Metropolitan Borough Council* [2003] UKHL 61 at [3].

*   *   *

So, when you ask yourself whether you are interested in the law, you don't need to restrict yourself to the narrow question of whether legal theory interests you. Of course, it very well might – jurisprudence is a fascinating topic in its own right. But, to practising lawyers, legal theory is usually of secondary relevance. The most interesting aspect of the law is in its application to your case.

Take another example:

> **Example**
>
> On 14 January 1956, Mrs Eileen Sayers was about to catch a bus from Essex to London with her husband. Before doing so, she went into the public toilets which were owned by the local council. She entered a cubicle which locked behind her and, to her dismay, she discovered that the handle on the inside was missing and she could not get out. In what seemed to be the only option left for her, she attempted to climb over the top of the cubicle, at the side where the toilet roll holder was positioned. She couldn't get over, and so started to climb back down. She placed her foot, and then her weight, on the toilet roll holder. The toilet roll spun round, and she fell and was injured. [12]

---

[12] See *Sayers v Harlow Urban District Council* [1958] 1 W.L.R. 623.

17

This case is a prime example of the interesting ways in which the law is applied to everyday life. It's a story which wouldn't be out of place in a magazine in a hairdresser's waiting area, but it is also a story which finds an important place in modern legal textbooks because of the legal questions surrounding Mrs Sayers' unfortunate experience in the toilet.

> The Judge found that the council was in breach of duty because it failed to provide a handle on the inside of the cubicle door. But the council argued that it was not to blame for the consequences which had befallen poor Mrs Sayers and was therefore not liable to make payment to her: it could not, it was said, have foreseen her actions; and she was to blame for her own unwise conduct.
>
> The Court of Appeal therefore had to look at whether the outcome had been the 'direct and natural consequence' of the Council's breach of duty.
>
> Happily for her, the Court considered that her actions were reasonable and foreseeable, and it held the council liable. But it found that she had also been a little careless in allowing her foot to rest on the rotating toilet roll, as a result of which she was entitled to recover damages for only 75% of her losses. She was made to bear the remaining 25% herself, as a result of her own carelessness.

*   *   *

As you will have seen from the above, as a barrister, you might find yourself asking such questions as:

> What are the relevant legal principles? Can I find some legal principle which will help my client to secure victory? Can I construe a statute to bolster my defence? What duties have the courts decided are required of architects, and have my architect clients complied with them?

> How should these principles be applied? Have the courts considered this contractual provision before, and what did they find it to mean? Which assets is my client entitled to after her divorce?

> What is the likelihood of success? How can I present advice as clearly as possible to my client? How best should I present my arguments to the Court?

If you are interested by these kinds of questions, and how the law can provide answers to them, then the law may well be for you.

Barristers, Solicitors and other legal professionals

Once you have decided that the law – or at least its application to the way we live and go about business – interests you, the next question to consider will be what type of role suits you best.

There have traditionally been two principal career paths: barristers and solicitors. There are, in fact, many other professionals in the legal sector, such as Chartered Legal Executives, Notaries and Paralegals, and you would be well-advised to spend some time familiarising yourself with these other roles. But the most frequent consideration for aspiring lawyers remains the choice between barrister and solicitor.

Barristers

In general terms, practising barristers are those who have carried out the relevant legal training, have been called to the Bar,[13] and hold a valid practising certificate. They are entitled to exercise rights of audience (that is to say, address a Court and perform advocacy) and advise clients on matters pertaining to their case.

The Bar is a diverse profession and it is difficult to generalise without unfairly omitting the work of others.

---

[13] A historic ceremony which is effectively the 'graduation' ceremony for BPTC students.

Barristers can be found in many roles and within varied organisations and structures.

Employed and Self-Employed

A common division is between employed and self-employed barristers.

This book is primarily directed at those considering the self-employed Bar (which, according to the Bar Council, comprises around 80% of barristers).[14]

But there are also, for example, large numbers of employed barristers, working either within and for the government, or in solicitors' firms or legal departments of companies or charities. Whilst being qualified in the same way as others at the Bar, the work of employed barristers is usually for one particular client, and often involves significantly less advocacy. They will typically be paid a salary rather than piecemeal for individual cases and items of work, may have greater stability and predictability in their finances and working hours, and will be supplied with cases to work on by their employer rather than having to source their own work. However, because they are employed, they will have less control over the type of work they do, how they do it, and when and what hours they will work.

At the self-employed Bar, on the other hand, barristers will be instructed by solicitors or lay-clients under

---

14   see   http://www.barcouncil.org.uk/about-the-bar/about-barristers/ where-do-barristers-practise

individual contracts in respect of each case taken on. The "instructions to counsel[15]" will usually ask the barrister to carry out a specific task.

Self-employed barristers typically have two types of input into cases:

> providing legal advice (both at early stages, and as the case progresses), and
> attending court to argue the case to the judge (and, in criminal cases, to the jury).

As always, if you have any doubts as to which would suit you best, you would be well-advised to try to undertake work experience with both self-employed and employed barristers.

Contracts – how barristers are engaged

Self-employed barristers will usually be engaged by multiple clients, often at the same time, and do so on separate, individual contracts pertaining to the particular instructions they are given.

In this regard, it is worth mentioning briefly that, whilst historically barristers did not carry out work under a contract and could not sue for their fees in court (they carried out work by an agreement which was binding in honour only), the regulatory framework was changed on 31

---

[15] "counsel" is a common way of referring to barristers.

January 2013. From that point onwards, barristers have worked under a personal contract for services.

Some sets of chambers have created their own standard terms and conditions on which their barristers will accept instructions. Likewise, the Bar Council has authorised a set of standard conditions which barristers can use in the absence of their own bespoke terms;[16] and various Bar associations have also collaborated in creating terms and conditions which can be used by their members.[17]

(As mentioned above, employed barristers will, on the other hand, usually be permanently engaged by one 'client' under a contract of employment.)

Instructions to Counsel

The scope of a barrister's work will be set out in the "instructions" received from the solicitor or client relating to the case in question.

The instructions will normally set out the details of the client and the case, what the barrister is required to do, and the timeframe in which it must be done. It will be up to you to ensure that you understand what is being requested, and

---

[16] A copy is available on the Bar Council website. The Bar Council has also produced a useful "Standard Contractual Terms Guide" which provides background information and details the various clauses found in the standard terms: see http://www.barcouncil.org.uk/media/182287/guide_to_contractual_terms.pdf

[17] See, for example, the standard terms agreed between COMBAR and City of London Law Society, a copy of which can be found on COMBAR's website.

that you are capable of carrying out the work by the deadline.

Typical instructions at the outset of a case may state something along the lines of, *"Counsel is instructed to advise on the merits of this case. The factual background is as follows..."* Prior to trial, a barrister may receive instructions setting out the background to the case and indicating that, *"Counsel is instructed to attend at the Royal Courts of Justice on 14 April and defend our client's position".*

Once instructions have been sent to you, there are only limited circumstances in which they can be refused. The 'cab rank rule' is a long-established professional obligation, currently formulated in rule C29 of the Code of Conduct.[18] With limited exceptions, this requires barristers to accept all instructions from professional clients as long as the barrister has the necessary expertise and availability and a proper fee is offered. This is an important principle in ensuring that all people have access to justice and are equal under the law: Barristers are not permitted to pick and choose which cases they think they may win, or which aligns with their own principles. In this way, barristers play an important role in upholding the rule of law, as the appropriate barristers will be available to everyone. It does mean, however, that you could find yourself in the difficult position of representing someone whose beliefs or values are contrary to your own, or someone who you consider to have acted shamefully. But it is not the role of the barrister

---

[18] See the Bar Standards Board Handbook, currently in its third edition (which came into force on 3 April 2017): see https://www.barstandardsboard.org.uk/media/1826458/bsb_hand book_31_march_2017.pdf

to play judge: instead you must have faith in the law, knowing that you are seeking the best outcome for your client within the confines of legitimate legal principle, and leaving an assessment of the merits to the Judge.

Mode of Work

The Bar can be a relatively solitary career. Whilst barristers usually operate from chambers in which there may be large numbers of other barristers, they are still self-employed and work largely alone. You will of course liaise and discuss cases with your instructing solicitor, but you are responsible for the task on which you have been instructed, and it is you who will carry the burden of persuading the Court of your client's position. You cannot delegate and you will not usually be instructed as part of a team. That suits many people very well: for those who enjoy immersing themselves in a task, rolling a problem around in their mind, and finding a bespoke solution, the responsibility and individuality can be liberating. For others, teamwork and co-operation is important, and sitting with your head in a book all day would be a nightmare.

The principal exception to this is where a junior barrister and 'silk' or Queen's Counsel ('QC') are both instructed on the same case. In such a scenario, the silk and junior work together, distributing workload as appropriate for the case. The silk usually performs the bulk of advocacy and determines the approach to be adopted whilst the junior carries out the more time-consuming but less skilled tasks (enabling a cost-saving for the client, whilst ensuring that the skills and experience of the more highly qualified practitioner are brought to bear on the decisive elements of the case).

Direct Access

Whilst barristers are usually (and historically) instructed by solicitors, they are now also permitted to undertake work directly for a lay-client without a solicitor forming part of the chain (provided the relevant training and certification has been obtained).

This is desirable for certain clients who may, for example, be unable to afford solicitors, or who wish for a discrete point of legal advice. It also provides a further way in which barristers can set up and market their business, depending on the work they wish to take on and the way in which they wish their business to operate.

Differences in Specialism

Until you have commenced a law degree or the Graduate Diploma in Law (GDL), it will probably be very difficult to have any realistic idea of what kind of specialism appeals to you. Even then, it can be difficult to get a proper feel for a job in the specialism without seeing it first-hand in work experience.

If you have had a previous career in (for example) IT or shipping, then chambers which specialise in IT or shipping law may be at the top of your list. Otherwise, try to get a broad idea of whether it is criminal, family or other civil work which interests you most. Keep a broadly open mind until you have studied the subjects and undertaken some work experience.

It is also useful to bear in mind that, even amongst those at the self-employed Bar, the hours and working environments differ enormously. Your area of specialism will, therefore, dictate not only what type of case you will be working on but also your manner of working.

Life as a criminal barrister, or a common law barrister, for example, will often have a heavy emphasis on court and advocacy. If you thrive off live debate and quick thinking, these would be well worth considering. Those practising in commercial, insurance, tax or construction law, on the other hand, spend a significant proportion of their time researching, advising and drafting documents in their office. If measured thought and analysis are your priority, these types of specialism may be more appropriate.

Selecting a suitable area of law is considered further in Chapter 10.

Solicitors

Solicitors, on the other hand, can be divided more broadly into contentious and non-contentious lawyers.

Non-contentious lawyers will rarely become involved in litigation and, instead, focus on advisory and transactional work.

contentious solicitors will be involved in disputes (which may or may not also involve barristers). Thus, solicitors involved in contentious work may pursue the arrest of vessels or aircraft, attend and represent their clients in mediations or tribunals and carry out any number of other dispute-related activities. They are also likely to be involved in the instructing of counsel and the conduct of litigation as a case proceeds to trial.

The role of solicitors is generally far more client-facing than that of barristers. They will be approached at the beginning of the dispute and will provide preliminary advice. They may deal with the matter themselves, or recommend that counsel be instructed. They will collect evidence and take witness statements; communicate with the other party (or their solicitors); carry out disclosure and review the other side's documents; instruct any necessary experts and generally co-ordinate the various elements of their client's case.

As a general rule, however, they will not carry out the advocacy on behalf of their client. This will usually be left to counsel. Where the case is complex or specialist in nature, they will also frequently seek advice from counsel at an early stage, on behalf of their client, on the merits of the case and on any protective steps which should be taken or any applications which should be made.

Over recent years, the distinction between barristers and solicitors has become a little more blurred.

As detailed above, barristers can now undertake additional training in order to accept instructions directly from the public and professionals (thereby eliminating the need for solicitors, who will not be instructed for that case). They can also now qualify to 'conduct the litigation' – which, in reality, means running the case from start to finish, including corresponding with the other party's solicitors, issuing and serving all the relevant court documents, and being on hand to advise and support the client as the claim progresses. These are roles which have traditionally been carried out by solicitors.

Likewise, solicitors have for many years been able to undertake additional training in advocacy, and take assessments, in order to qualify for 'higher rights of audience'.[19]   This means that they will be entitled to exercise rights of audience – address judges – in the higher courts in much the same way as barristers.

Nevertheless, this overlap has, to date, remained fairly limited. Many barristers feel that conducting litigation would unduly restrict their capacity to carry out the 'usual' activities traditionally associated with barristers, and have no desire to do so. Their time would rapidly be consumed with correspondence and client management, and their focus on legal analysis and advocacy would be correspondingly reduced. Likewise, solicitors have often selected that career path for the client contact, problem-solving and analytical nature typically associated with the

---

[19] Access by solicitors to other tribunals is not new: they have full rights of audience in Tribunals, Coroners Courts, Magistrates Courts, County Courts, the Family Court and European Courts. An application for civil higher rights of audience allows them also to appear in civil proceedings in the Crown Court, High Court, Court of Appeal and Supreme Court.

solicitors' profession, and the idea of carrying out the advocacy in addition is not something which appeals.

Other Legal Professionals

There are a number of other legal professional roles which might be of interest and further information on these can be obtained from the Law Society's website.[20]

For present purposes, you ought to be aware of two:

- Chartered Legal Executives: These are individuals who have trained and qualified in certain areas of law and who can advise and represent clients. They are regulated by the Chartered Institute of Legal Executives, may be employed or self-employed, and perform similar tasks to solicitors but in a narrower field. They have the option of subsequently undertaking further legal qualification to become a solicitor.

- Paralegals: These are often individuals who have carried out some legal training (such as a law degree, GDL) and who then work in a supporting role to solicitors. They may carry out research, draft documents and administer case files, but will not give advice to clients.

---

[20] See https://www.lawsociety.org.uk/for-the-public/legal-professionals-who-does-what

*   *   *

In the end, after putting some serious thought into what interests you most, go and apply for work experience.

Chapter 3: Chambers and Clerks – how things work.

Barristers' chambers come in all shapes and sizes. They can range from a sole practitioner, or a couple of individuals operating together, to a large set of over 100 barristers. They can specialise in one distinct area of law, such as intellectual property law or medical negligence, or offer services in a number of complementary (or even entirely unrelated) disciplines.

This diversity stems from the inherent freedom which pervades life at the Bar. A barrister has the freedom to set him- or herself up in chambers of their own choosing, to suit their practice and to work towards goals in the way he/she considers best. This can enable you to make a virtue of your difference.

The historic model

The historic model is built around a senior barrister, a Queen's Counsel (known as a "QC"), who is the head of the chambers, and a number of junior barristers working in the same premises under the watchful eye of the QC.

In this way, the juniors benefit from the experience and reputation of the QC (gaining work which comes into chambers as a result of his/her name), and are also on hand to act in a junior role to the QC where the QC requires assistance.

Movement towards growth

This 'petite' historic model has become increasingly rare. Most (although by no means all) successful chambers over recent decades, and particularly those based in London, have found strength in numbers. Indeed some chambers have now merged to provide 'branches' and offerings in multiple cities under the same chambers brand.

With a larger offering, they are able to focus on building a reputation and presence more widely; they can offer specialist expertise in a wider number of fields; they are more likely to have barristers available to accept instructions when they come in, which enables relationships with solicitors to be strengthened; and, when necessary, they are more likely to have 'teams' or pairs of barristers available to accept instructions together on larger cases.

These larger chambers will, therefore, tend to have a number of QCs, many juniors and an administration team (including clerks and other staff) keeping things in order.

Why belong to chambers?

The attachment of barristers to a set of chambers often gives rise to misunderstandings amongst non-lawyers, who sometimes think of barristers as being employed by chambers. Not so. They remain self-employed and solely responsible for their own work at all times.

So why do barristers sacrifice a certain autonomy and expend part of their income on belonging to a set of chambers? In short, it is a successful and cost-effective business model which has a proven track record over many years. It continues to be a useful tool for many purposes:

> ➢ Barristers can collectively build a reputation for high quality work (or not, as the case may be!). This enables 'sets' of chambers to be ranked in the legal directories and to attract work from solicitors who have not previously instructed them.

> ➢ Chambers will also often build a reputation in a particular field of expertise. Accordingly, when a solicitor requires advice in, say, a property or planning dispute, he/she will be able to instruct a barrister at a specialist set knowing that the barrister will have expertise in that field, even when the solicitor hasn't come across that barrister previously.

> ➢ Where a case is sufficiently large, valuable or complex, clients may wish to instruct a team of barristers, or a QC with a junior. In cases which are document heavy, this type of instruction is

particularly common, since it will be more cost-effective for the client to pay a junior to carry out the documentary 'leg work', and then to pay the QC to approve final drafts, give advice and perform the advocacy. This type of delegation is common in other industries, and takes place without a second thought. When instructing the Bar, however, it needs to be specifically sanctioned by clients in light of the personal contract for services by which a client instructs a particular barrister.

➤ Administrative costs (including the provision of clerks and other administrative staff) can be shared, thereby saving costs and reducing the financial outgoings of individual barristers.

➤ The cost of premises are shared, again reducing the outgoings of any one barrister. Indeed, for those barristers based in central London, the cost of renting premises, were they to do so individually, may be prohibitive.

➤ Barristers can receive support from others in chambers. When working together in such close proximity, strong bonds will often form between barristers. A barrister who finds him or herself in difficulty, either on a personal basis or professionally, may find support and advice from others in chambers.

How Chambers operate

As with so much at the Bar, there is no standard model by which all chambers operate. Much will depend on the size of the chambers, the number of staff employed by the barristers, and the type of work undertaken.

Let us begin with what chambers generally share in common.

> Chambers will almost universally comprise a number of barristers grouping together to pool their resources and share expenditure.

> Barristers will pay certain funds or 'contributions' into the chambers 'pot' which will be used to pay for communal outgoings, such as the cost of premises, services (such as water, electricity, telephone, internet), maintenance and cleaners.

> You can typically expect a set of chambers to employ a number of clerks and, possibly, some other administrative staff, to oversee the work coming in and to collect payment of fees for work done.

> Chambers will often also share research materials. There may be an internal chambers library comprising the most frequently used practitioner works. There may also be a group subscription to online legal resources, such as Westlaw or Lexis Nexis.

How, then, do they often differ? The differences tend to be in the detail:

➤ The method by which barristers contribute financially to the operation of chambers is a common difference. This will usually be set out in the founding document or constitution of chambers; or it may be found in a jointly-agreed procedure document. Some chambers charge barristers a 'rental' fee based on the size of their room, or how many people they share with; others charge a fixed fee. Some will charge a fixed percentage of the barrister's income. The financial contribution to chambers can vary wildly from set to set. This information is usually considered by chambers to be highly sensitive and confidential and will not be published online. It is unlikely to be something which you will be able to factor in to your decision to apply to a particular set.

➤ Room allocation can also vary from chambers to chambers. Some sets will have sufficient space to allow each barrister to have their own private office. Others operate room-sharing arrangements; and certain sets with an emphasis on low financial contributions, or where space is tight, operate a hot-desking arrangement.

➤ The number of administrative staff likewise differs. As can be expected, sets with more barristers will usually employ more clerks and admin staff. Those with a focus on cost reduction will have fewer.

> Finally, it goes without saying that the atmosphere at chambers can differ considerably. A set is the sum of its constituent parts, and will often reflect the personalities and work ethic of its members. Some chambers will be stuffy and old-fashioned, some may feel excessively relaxed, and some will achieve a happy medium. Try to use your work experience to play at being 'Goldilocks'.

The Clerks

The clerks' room is usually the administrative hub of a set of chambers. Clerks are not qualified lawyers and usually have no legal training but, instead, act as agents for the barristers in the administration and management of their practices.[21]

The clerks are usually responsible for bringing in new work to chambers, distributing instructions that come in, and negotiating fees. They will enter into contracts with solicitors or lay clients for the provision of services on your behalf, under authority delegated by you.

Accordingly, a barrister's relationship with his/her clerk can be one of the most intimate you will find outside a family. Your clerk will probably know the precise details of your income, your workload, your diary, your evening and weekend engagements, and where you are going on holiday.

---

[21] Their professional body is the *Institute of Barristers' Clerks*: see https://www.ibc.org.uk/ for more information.

There should be a high level of trust and confidence between barrister and clerk. You will have discussions with your clerks concerning your income and fee level; what it is appropriate to be charging in your area of work and for your level of call;[22] and what kind of fee is suitable on a particular case in hand. If they are doing their jobs correctly, your clerks will also be aware of the general market rates being charged by other sets and will price you appropriately without underselling you. They might take a view as to when a discount is appropriate, in order to generate goodwill for the future.

It is also a necessarily collaborative relationship. When you are starting out on your career at the Bar, without existing professional connections and work-streams, your clerk will be the one to channel work to you and to point you in the right direction. You may also attend marketing and networking events together, in order to build up contacts with solicitors and lay clients, and to generate new work-streams.

Likewise, even when you have established a strong reputation and sufficient contacts to ensure regular and repeat instructions directly to you, your clerk will be the contact point for those instructions and will manage your diary. If there are timing and deadline difficulties, your clerk

---

[22] A barrister's level of call relates to the time which has passed since they were called to the Bar. So, for someone who was called in 2010, their level of call would be the number of years between 2010 and the present date. It is a rough (and somewhat imprecise) way of measuring the seniority of a barrister.

will attempt to adjust the diary or negotiate movement to deadlines to facilitate the acceptance of instructions.

It is also worth remembering that the barrister is not the only one with a reputation to build. A clerk will build up his/her own reputation in the business, and will make personal contacts with solicitors. Thus, if the clerk recommended a particular barrister to a solicitor with whom he/she had built up a rapport, damage could be done to that relationship if the barrister underperformed. Similarly, if the clerk was to move to a different set of chambers, that individual would take his/her knowledge and contact list, to the benefit of the new employer.

In terms of remuneration, the clerks' pay may be based on the income of their barristers, thereby giving incentive to bring more work into chambers. A clerk may, for example, be paid a percentage of the fee earned by the barrister; or may be incentivised by a bonus based on performance or chambers earnings to be added to the base salary.

The clerks are also generally responsible for the timely collection of fees. Some chambers employ designated 'fee clerks' whose job is solely focussed on collection of fees. Other chambers have administrative staff who invoice clients and deal with payments. But many chambers retain the traditional model by which the clerks, having negotiated the fee in the first place, will subsequently invoice and chase for payment.

Clerks at certain sets were, in the past, somewhat unfairly viewed and treated as subordinates. In certain quarters this unfortunate view persists, but, as can be seen from the above discussion, in a modern set, a clerk's relationship with a barrister is one of mutual respect, trust and collaboration.

Chapter 4: the Inns of Court

The four Inns of Court are unusual institutions, with little by way of comparison in other professions. Their functions have developed over centuries, but they have remained as centres of education and accommodation. They are important in the development of, and support given to, a barrister through to his/her Call to the Bar and thereafter.

The origins of the Inns of Court can be traced back to around the 13th and 14th centuries. Inner and Middle Temple began as societies or groupings of lawyers who congregated and occupied the land originally belonging to the Knights Templar who built the round Temple Church by the Thames in the middle of the 12th century. Likewise, Inns developed around Holborn at a similar time, possibly as a result of a decree of Henry III on 2 December 1234 to the effect that no body providing legal education should be located in the City of London.

There were originally many more Inns than the four which remain today, and which are known as Inner Temple, Middle Temple, Gray's Inn and Lincoln's Inn. They were set up, on a similar basis to the Oxford and Cambridge colleges, to provide education, accommodation and dining, and their nomenclature of 'Inn' appears to derive from the hospitality offered. Over time, they attracted a wide range of individuals, not solely lawyers or those interested in practising law, and, by the 16th century, the Inns were flourishing with many statesmen and renowned figures counting among their ranks.[23]

The Inns are now run by 'Benchers', who are senior practitioners and members of the judiciary. Still providing education, dining and accommodation, though on a more restricted and focussed basis, they retain the profession's connection to its history whilst also looking forward, expanding the facilities available, and increasing access, to the Bar.

They still fulfil an important role for those embarking on a career at the Bar. In order to qualify as a barrister, you will be required to participate in training offered by the Inns known as 'qualifying sessions'. You must also be a member of, and called to the Bar by, one of the Inns in order to satisfy the regulatory requirements and to practise as a barrister.

Funding

A significant role played by the Inns of Court in the life of their student members relates to their funding provision for the Common Professional Examination (CPE) / Graduate Diploma in Law (GDL) and Bar Professional Training Course (BPTC).

---

[23] For further information, see Havery's *History of the Middle Temple* (2011).

The Inns offer a wide range of scholarships, providing financial assistance for selected applicants. For the GDL/CPE, the closing date for applications is usually the May immediately preceding the start of the course. For the BPTC, the closing date for such awards is usually around November in the year before the BPTC starts.

Reference should be made to the individual websites of the four Inns well in advance of the deadline for applications, and both the level of funding and the criteria applied by the different Inns may be something you wish to take into account when making your initial application to join. In this regard, the different Inns adopt different procedures for awarding funding. They will also have different criteria, different sums on offer, and different numbers of applicants. Your chances of obtaining funding may be impacted by your financial status or parents' income; your academic ability; and performance in assessments or interview. Spend some time working out which will be best for your circumstances.

Training

The Inns also provide elements of training at all stages of practice, both pre- and post-qualification.

By way of example, in order to be called to the Bar, all BPTC students have to complete 12 "qualifying sessions", which are provided by the Inn of which they are a member. These qualifying sessions historically consisted of attendance at dinners with members at the Inn, but now also include, amongst other things, lectures on legal topics, residential advocacy weekends away, and ethics courses.

Mentors

The Inns each run mentoring or sponsorship schemes, by which barrister members agree to mentor a student allocated by the Inn. Where possible, the designated barrister will practise in the area of law of interest to the student.

The mentoring schemes are yet another valuable opportunity to discuss the realities of life and work at the Bar. There is no pressure to 'perform' for your mentor, who is there to encourage and advise you rather than judge or criticise. You may also wish to ask your mentor to give you any useful tips or comments on your CV, or on which chambers might be most appropriate for you to apply to.

Continuing benefits

The continuing relevance of the Inns to barristers after qualification is variable.

In the first three years' of practice, barristers must complete a certain amount and type of continuing professional development (CPD). This is often fulfilled by attending residential weekends away, organised by the Inns, in which more experienced members will provide training to the juniors.

Dinners, social events and educational opportunities form a large part of the Inns' calendars. These can provide a good way of getting to know colleagues or members of the judiciary, and also provide an entertaining evening for family and friends.

The Inns have extensive libraries which are available for the use of members. These include historic and current legal volumes, as well as online resources.

Most of the buildings around Temple, in which barristers' chambers are based, are owned by the Inns and rented out to barristers. Likewise, the Inns rent out a limited number of private rooms to members who need short or long term residential accommodation.

Finally, the Inns possess various car parking facilities around their buildings which are used by members (for a fee).

Outreach

As part of their programme of events, the Inns perform outreach roles, going to schools/universities and providing insight into the profession. These provide yet more valuable opportunities to meet and speak with barristers and members of the judiciary, to determine whether this is a suitable profession for you and, if so, in which area. They are also excellent opportunities to see the warmth and collegiality within the profession.

Choosing an Inn

Students often become overly concerned about which Inn to join, and fire an array of questions at barristers concerning which Inn is best.

In truth, there is little between them, and membership of a particular Inn is unlikely to make any substantial difference to you after your initial couple of years of training. Even during training, the opportunities provided are almost identical, and the ultimate decision usually comes down to two questions:

> ➤ first, which Inn has the most beneficial funding and scholarship system for my circumstances?
> ➤ second, do any of the little idiosyncrasies, the facilities or the aesthetics of an Inn particularly appeal to me (bearing in mind that you will be able to use most facilities of all Inns anyway)?

The Inns hold regular open days and outreach events, and their Education and Training departments are open and friendly. If travel is easy for you, aim to visit the four Inns early to take a brief look at them; research their funding systems; and then join.

Whilst it is compulsory to join the Inn before the May of the year in which you commence the BPTC, the earlier you join the better in order that you can sign up to the various activities and events hosted by the Inn and start building your knowledge.

Chapter 5: Getting to know the profession

Perhaps more so than most other professions, the Bar can appear distant and difficult to penetrate. To those on the outside, it can seem impossible to get to know barristers and to get a feel for their working life. It may also seem that there is less of an active push towards outreach and openness than one would expect to see in comparable companies hungry for new talent. As a group of self-employed individuals, this is probably not surprising.

But do not despair.

Opportunities to meet with barristers are not too difficult to come by, provided that you know the right places to look.

Before University

There is no doubt that, if you are wanting to get to know the profession, the most difficult time to do so is before you have started at university.

Whilst irritating, there is a reasonable explanation for this.

Because barristers are self-employed and are paid only for the work they carry out, any time they spend on non-work related activities will directly hit their pocket. The Bar is not, on the whole, a selfish profession, and there is a lot of goodwill towards aspiring barristers. Indeed, as time progresses, you will find that much of the training given to you, and many events at which you are hosted, will be done by barristers without any expectation of reward or remuneration. This goodwill stems from the desire of barristers to help those who are genuinely interested in a career at the Bar discover more about the profession and to achieve their goals. But barristers have little interest in simply giving someone another entry to stick on their CV. They will, therefore, often restrict their participation in non-remunerative activities to those activities which are likely to yield actual, positive results for the intended beneficiaries.

In short, the more genuinely interested someone is, the more likely they are to go on to pursue a career at the Bar. The more likely they are to pursue a career at the Bar, the more likely they are to benefit from the barrister's time and, in such circumstances, the barrister is less likely to have wasted his/her time.

One way of demonstrating this genuine interest is by continuing down the path of legal education. As a person progresses down this path, they become increasingly likely to go ahead in pursuing a career at the Bar. Pre-university students will, by nature of the early stage they are at, struggle to demonstrate a genuine interest in, or anticipation of, a career at the Bar. There are, however, still ways in which they can do so: by attending court to sit in the public gallery during trials; by undertaking work experience with solicitors' firms; by reading legal books. With something relevant to talk about, any covering letter seeking work experience will then be far better received than if sent by someone going in without any prior knowledge.

At University

Once you have arrived at university, a broad range of options become available to you. You can begin applying for work experience in earnest – and you would be well-advised to do as much as you can.

But do not overlook, in addition to work experience,[24] the other opportunities to meet members of the profession and to explore the workings of the Bar.

> ➢ The law societies of many of the major universities will arrange events, either with individual chambers or with the Inns of Court. These can include dinners, lectures, and visits to the Inns or chambers. They are to be encouraged, not least because they give opportunities to speak informally with members of chambers about what their life at the Bar entails, and what you can expect.

> ➢ If you are a law student, you are also able to join one of the Inns of Court from the second year of your undergraduate law degree onwards, or once you

---

[24] Which is discussed in detail in chapter 8.

have a confirmed place on the GDL / CPE. The Inns of Court arrange regular events, including dinners (both at the Inns and at universities) and lectures.

➢ Certain chambers will advertise 'open days' for students considering a career at the Bar. These are excellent opportunities to visit a set of chambers, meet some of their barristers and hear more about the types of work they carry out, without any of the pressure of an individual mini-pupillage (although they should be used in addition to mini-pupillage rather than as a substitute!).

➢ There are various associations which you can join as a student. YIAG (the Young International Arbitration Group), for example, hosts regular events at which both students and professionals attend.[25]

After University

Many of the same opportunities continue once you have finished your university education. Thus, provided you have joined an Inn of Court, you can attend dinners and events which it hosts. Chambers open days will be equally available to you and likewise in respect of joining professional associations.

---

[25] See http://www.lcia.org/membership/yiag/young_international_ arbitration_group.aspx for more information.

Your BPTC / GDL / CPE provider may also host events or have links in place with chambers or Inns of Court for dinners, lectures or networking.

As detailed in Chapter 4 above, you will be required to complete 12 "qualifying sessions" before you can be Called to the Bar. Qualifying sessions include a variety of activities, hosted or arranged by the Inns of Court, such as dining in Hall, lectures, advocacy workshops and residential weekends. In addition to being a regulatory requirement, they are an excellent means of getting to know other members of the profession.

Chapter 6: The Academic Stage: University, the Common Professional Examination (CPE) and the Graduate Diploma in Law (GDL)

The Bar is a challenging profession, which imposes high intellectual demands on its members and requires strong analytical and organisational skills.

In order to qualify as a barrister, you are therefore required, first, to pass an academic stage of qualification. This consists of either a "Qualifying Law Degree" or a degree in another subject together with the Common Professional Examination (CPE) or an approved Graduate Diploma in Law (GDL) course.[26]

There are seven key or 'core' foundation subjects which must be covered in a Qualifying Law Degree or CPE/GDL course order to qualify for a career at the Bar:

---

[26] For further information, see https://www.barstandardsboard .org.uk/qualifying-as-a-barrister/current-requirements/academic-stage/

- Public Law (including Constitutional Law, Administrative Law and Human Rights)
- Law of the European Union
- Criminal Law
- The Law of Contract
- The Law of Torts and Restitution
- Property Law
- Equity and the Law of Trusts

These provide the basis for an academic legal education in order to qualify for the Bar or as a solicitor.

The academic stage is intended to ensure that prospective barristers have a basic, all-round understanding of the legal framework in England and Wales, and to provide a platform from which the Bar Professional Training Course (BPTC) can be undertaken.

Law Degree or other degree plus GDL/CPE?

Most chambers have no preference between a law degree and a non-law degree plus 'conversion'.

The real advantage of a law degree is in the additional time you will be able to spend absorbing and understanding the law and legal framework. Thus, in addition to the seven 'core' subjects, you will be able to undertake study in an array of other optional modules. If you have a firm idea of the area of law in which you wish to practise, these modules are a good 'entry' into the subject area.

On the other hand, a non-law degree enables you to expand your field of study and, importantly, spend your time at university working on something that truly interests you. Provided this is an academic subject which will help to build the skills needed for a career in law, you should be in no way disadvantaged by undertaking a non-law degree followed by the conversion course.

Expected Grades

When applying for pupillage, candidates will be expected to have achieved (or be predicted to achieve) excellent grades at university and on the professional training courses. This is an easy way for an assessor to ascertain your capabilities and will usually form the basis of the first 'sift' of applications.

The minimum requirement for completion of the academic stage is a lower second class (2:2) UK Honours degree or equivalent. That said, when it comes to applications to chambers for pupillage, a 2:2 will rarely be sufficient to get you through the first round.

Most chambers indicate their selection criteria on their websites, to which you should always refer before making any application. For the top chambers, you are unlikely to be considered without an upper second class or first class degree and (if the degree was not in law) strong performance in the GDL/CPE.

That notwithstanding, in the event that you have underperformed, reasonable personal mitigation and justification will almost always be taken into account. You should be upfront and honest about any failure to achieve the relevant chambers' desired criteria, and provide a clear and concise explanation where appropriate in your application.

Undergraduate Education

Selection of the appropriate university for you to attend is a highly personal decision, with many influencing factors such as reputation, location, size, subject availability, cost, and extra-curricular opportunities.

Keep the reputation and standing of the university high in your list of priorities. Many chambers have a high proportion of Oxford and Cambridge graduates among their recent tenants, not because they have some bias towards Oxbridge, but because those universities are amongst the highest ranked in the world and are, therefore, highly competitive, attracting some of the best available talent. But there are a number of other exceptional universities in the UK which also attract the attention of leading chambers. The Russell Group of universities[27] is a good place to begin your research. A tenancy committee will need to have confidence in the quality of your academic background and degree. For the best chance to succeed in obtaining pupillage, you should be aiming for the best university your grades will get you into.

---

[27] See http://russellgroup.ac.uk/about/our-universities

Universities frequently have a number of law-related societies, and hold events such as mooting, debating, and guest lectures by eminent legal speakers. These are unlikely to be a decisive factor in your decision on which university to attend, but whether you are undertaking a law degree or a degree in a different subject, take advantage of all the opportunities that your university offers you.

The LNAT

The National Admissions Test for Law (abbreviated to 'LNAT') is an aptitude test, centrally set, which is required by certain universities. You should check with your preferred university to ascertain whether, for your year of entry, they require the LNAT to be taken.[28]

The LNAT does not test your knowledge of the law, but is intended to test your skills with particular focus on verbal reasoning, understanding and interpretation of information, inductive and deductive reasoning, and analysis of information.

The test currently lasts 2¼ hours, and is split into two sections: Section A consists of 42 multiple-choice questions; and Section B requires a response to one of three essay questions.

To register, you must create an online account on the LNAT website and choose an appointment slot at a test centre of your choice. You must pay in advance to sit the LNAT

---

[28] See further http://www.lnat.ac.uk/what-is-lnat/do-i-need-to-sit-the-test/

(pricing for the year 2016/17 being £50 or £70 for UK/EU test centres and non-EU test centres respectively. Certain bursaries are available for those unable to fund the cost.

Further information can be found at http://www.lnat.ac.uk.

Graduate Diploma in Law / Common Professional Examination

The GDL and CPE are the primary options available to graduates whose degree was not in law. There is relatively little difference between the two (the GDL providing a formal diploma at completion), given that the course is primarily taken up by satisfaction of the foundation subjects. There is no disadvantage to taking one over the other.

The courses last one year (two years if taken part time), and cover the core foundation subjects required to be called to the Bar, together with a small amount of other legal teaching. Whilst this 'fast track' law training will not ultimately give the same breadth in legal knowledge as would be achieved through a full law degree, chambers tend to express no preference between the two.

It is also relatively immaterial which course provider you select for the GDL / CPE in terms of pupillage applications, as chambers tend to be fairly neutral in this regard. You will, however, be expected to obtain a Merit or above.

A number of institutions offer the CPE or GDL, including those located in Aberystwyth, Birmingham, Bournemouth, Birmingham, Bradford, Brighton, Bristol, Cambridge,

Cardiff, Carlisle, Chester, Glasgow, Guildford, Huddersfield, Keele, Leeds, Liverpool, London, Leicester, Manchester, Newcastle, Norwich, Nottingham, Oxford, Plymouth, Preston, Redditch, Sheffield, Stoke on Trent, Swansea and Wolverhampton. An up-to-date list can be seen on the Solicitors' Regulation Authority (SRA) website at http://www.sra.org.uk/students/conversion-courses/cpe-gdl-providers.page

Applications are made centrally online through the Central Applications Board (CAB) at www.lawcabs.ac.uk

You should obtain copies of the prospectuses of the schools which interest you; attend their open days; read reviews of those who have studied there previously; look at any published data on success rates.

Post-Graduate Academic Education

In light of the level of competition, many candidates for pupillage will seek to undertake post-graduate study at university. This can be useful in a number of situations:

> When you have underperformed on your degree at undergraduate level, and are currently unable to demonstrate strong (or sufficiently strong) academic ability;

> When your preferred chambers has a track record in preferring more mature candidates with a post-graduate qualification;

> ➤ When your undergraduate degree was not in law and you would prefer a longer, more thorough, legal education than that provided by the GDL.

> ➤ When you intend to apply to specialist sets who express a preference for candidates with wider academic experience in their field of expertise. Do not, however, assume that such experience is required simply because the set specialises in a particular type of law. To practise in the field of engineer's negligence, for example, it is not necessary to train as an engineer!

You should think carefully before embarking upon further education. It will often be extremely costly to undertake the qualification and you will also be postponing the time at which you will start to generate an income.

Provided that a candidate is able to demonstrate a strong record of academic results, many chambers will not differentiate between applicants with one degree and those with multiple. It is the skill set, and the ability to learn and adapt, that is most important. Having already studied the basic foundation subjects (as required through the 'academic requirements'), any further specialist substantive law can usually be acquired during the steep learning curve of pupillage.

Pre-University Education

You will be expected to demonstrate a strong track record of academic achievement, both in order to obtain a place at university and also when you come to apply for pupillage.

However, your specific subject choices are less prescribed.

Prior to embarking on your A-Levels, you should, of course, check the requirements of your desired universities in case there are any mandatory subjects. Provided you undertake recognised academic subjects, such as Maths, History, Geography, English, Languages and Sciences, there are unlikely to be any issues arising with your pre-university qualifications when it comes to pupillage applications.

The position is even less strict when it comes to GCSEs or equivalent. Again, provided that you have a good number of academic subjects amongst your selected subjects, the most important focus is on the achieved grades, in order to demonstrate a history of ability, motivation and achievement.

Second Careers

For those who have already had a career, and are moving to the Bar slightly later in life, the pure academic profile will be of slightly reduced importance. Of course, it remains important in showing the intellectual capacity of the candidate, but applicants will often be able to demonstrate such skills through other means as well. In these cases, the more difficult task for applicants will be to isolate and deconstruct the evidence needed to demonstrate that they have these abilities and skill sets.

Nevertheless, you will still have to qualify in the seven foundation subjects detailed above, and that can provide evidence of academic ability where necessary.

Keeping an eye to the future

The academic stage of qualification is an excellent time to begin narrowing your focus in terms of specialist practice areas. If you have not already decided which area you intend to pursue, your study of the foundation subjects should shed some light on what interests you most.

If you are undertaking a law degree, you will have the additional luxury of space in the curriculum in which to take additional modules in other areas of law. Popular topics include Family Law, Intellectual Property, Commercial, Employment, Landlord & Tenant, Administrative, Information Technology and Tax. There are many more, and you should explore them thoroughly before selecting an option, as they can be a valuable addition to a pupillage (or mini-pupillage) application to a chambers practising in that specialist area.

Chapter 7: The Vocational Stage: the Bar Professional Training Course (BPTC)

Having completed the academic stage, you will next be required to complete the vocational stage of training – the Bar Professional Training Course (the BPTC).[29]

The BPTC was started in 2010, having replaced the Bar Vocational Course (BVC) following a review. It is intended to provide an entirely separate skill set and understanding of the Bar to that acquired in the academic stage: in addition to intellectual ability, barristers require knowledge of legal procedure and evidence, ethics, and types of dispute resolution. Thus, students will undertake study in, amongst others:

> ➤ Professional Ethics
> ➤ Civil Litigation, Evidence and Remedies
> ➤ Criminal Litigation, Evidence and Sentencing

---

[29] Further information can be found at https://www.barstandardsboard.org.uk/qualifying-as-a-barrister/current-requirements/bar-professional-training-course/

They are also required to demonstrate competence in necessary skills, such as advocacy.[30]

The BPTC can be taken on a full- or part-time basis, the former lasting for one year and the latter for two (although not all providers currently offer the part-time course).

Most chambers will expect you to attain at least a grade of Very Competent.

Entry Requirements

There are some basic entry requirements[31] which must be satisfied in order to be considered for a place on the BPTC:

- ✓ Applicants must have satisfied the academic stage requirements.
- ✓ Applicants must be fluent in English.
- ✓ Applicants must pass the Bar Course Aptitude Test (the BCAT). This is an online test consisting of 60 multiple choice questions, which tests students' critical thinking and reasoning. It costs £150 if taken in the EU or £170 if taken outside the EU.

---

[30] For full details of the course specification and requirements, reference should be made to the BPTC Handbook produced by the Bar Standards Board at: https://www.barstandardsboard.org.uk/media/1791359/bptc_handbook_2016-17.pdf

[31] See https://www.barstandardsboard.org.uk/qualifying-as-a-barrister/current-requirements/bar-professional-training-course/how-to-apply-for-the-bptc/

✓ Before registration on a BPTC course, applicants must be members of an Inn of Court.[32]

Applications

Applications are made through the online application system at https://www.barsas.com. There is no provision for application by post and applications cannot be submitted directly to course providers.

Current providers of the BPTC are:

- BPP Law School in London, Leeds, Manchester and Birmingham;
- The University of Law in London, Birmingham and Leeds;
- The City Law School (formerly Inns of Court School of Law), London
- Manchester Metropolitan University
- Nottingham Law School
- The University of Northumbria, Newcastle
- The University of the West of England, Bristol
- Cardiff Law School.[33]

As with the GDL/CPE, chambers have no real preference when it comes to BPTC providers. Obtain copies of the

---

[32] In respect of which, see Chapter 4.
[33] For further details, see the Bar Standards Board website at https://www.barstandardsboard.org.uk/qualifying-as-a-barrister/current-requirements/bar-professional-training-course/bptc-providers/

prospectuses of the providers which interest you; attend their open days; read reviews of those who have studied there previously; and look at any published data on success rates. Whilst by no means necessary, you may also think about applying to a provider close to the sets of chambers to which you intend to apply, in order to be able to carry out work experience, attend court or meet practitioners.

Funding

As detailed in Chapter 4, varying levels of funding for the BPTC, including scholarships, are on offer from the Inns of Court. This source of funding is by no means guaranteed: limited funds are available and many students miss out entirely. Others will only receive a contribution towards the total costs, rather than a full indemnity.

For those lucky enough already to have secured a pupillage, their chambers may also give an award towards the BPTC, or (more frequently) may permit their future pupil to 'draw down' part of their pupillage awards[34] early, during the BPTC. This varies from chambers to chambers, and is usually mentioned in the Pupillage section of their website.

If neither of those sources of funding are available, students may have to fall back on savings and investments, bank loans and/or other forms of support. There are a number of banks which will offer loans for vocational courses, but you should ensure that you are fully apprised of the risks in

---

[34] Your pupillage award is the sum you are paid by your chambers for carrying out pupillage; what you might think of as your salary.

taking out loans. In particular, you should be particularly cautious in seeking funding from a lender if you have not yet secured a pupillage and have no plan for how it will be repaid.

Is the BPTC right for me?

You should think carefully before enrolling on the BPTC course. It is an expensive undertaking (course fees for the 2017/2018 intake ranged from around £13,000 to around £19,000) and the Bar Standards Board ('BSB') has published information to the effect that, whilst around 1400 students take the Bar Course every year, the number of pupillages typically offered is around only 433.[35]

That said, if you have carefully considered the risk and your likely prospects of success, and remain determined to pursue a career at the Bar, successful completion of the BPTC remains, for the moment, a necessary step.

The Future of the BPTC

Whilst the BPTC has been required, in its current form, since 2010, this general approach to vocational training has long been criticised. It is expensive (and is often criticised as failing to offer value for money), it can be slow

---

[35] Reference should be made to the Bar Standards Board's 'Health Warning' at: https://www.barstandardsboard.org.uk/media/1768892/health_warning_for_prospective_bar_professional_training_course_students.pdf

(particularly since classes comprise people of varying abilities), and large numbers of students enrolling on courses have no prospect of obtaining a pupillage at the end of it given the high competition.

Accordingly, a consultation was launched by the Bar Standards Board in October 2016, relating to the future of training for the Bar and the routes to authorisation. A number of alternatives were put forward, most of which alter fundamentally the way in which training would be given.

The proposal favoured by most practising barristers was the option suggested by the Council for the Inns of Court, which would lead to splitting the vocational training into two:

Part 1 would consist of the knowledge-based part of the course (principally rules and practice of civil litigation, criminal proceedings and sentencing), and students would be able to prepare by private study or tuition given by providers at their option. This would be followed by an examination set centrally by the BSB.

Part 2, which could only be commenced upon satisfactory completion of Part 1, would consist of the skills-based requirements, which would be undertaken at an approved provider. It is thought that this would considerably decrease the cost to students.

However, other options were also put forward, some of which practitioners consider would be extremely difficult to implement.

In March 2017, the BSB decided to authorise a number of training routes for future qualification.[36] The outcome and detail is yet to be finalised, and the impact it will have on training is unknown. You would be well-advised to keep an eye out for future developments, although it is thought that, whichever proposal comes to be accepted, it will not be implemented before 2018/19.

---

[36] See https://www.barstandardsboard.org.uk/media-centre/press-releases-and-news/bsb-announces-decision-on-the-future-of-bar-training and https://www.barstandardsboard.org.uk/media/1825162/032317_fbt_-_policy_statement_version_for_publication.pdf

Chapter 8: Mini-pupillage and other work experience

Work experience, work experience, work experience. Its importance cannot be underestimated.

Reading and research can only take you so far. Until you have seen people actually doing the job, and looked closely at the work they do in the practice area, the image you have may be very far from reality.

This is of course the case with any job, but it is particularly acute with the Bar. If you still have an image of an old, bewigged barrister gliding into court, his black gown wafting behind him as he throws his papers onto the table in front of him and begins a silver-tongued, tear-inducing cross-examination, then the reality of advocacy – which tends to be far less dramatic – may come as a surprise. So too may the amount of time spent on reading, marking up and labelling your papers, and preparation.

It is therefore absolutely vital to undertake as much work experience as you can get your hands on – mini-pupillages with barristers, vacation schemes at solicitors' firms, marshalling with judges in court, and any other ad hoc placements which may prove informative. These are discussed in turn below.

Even getting work experience can be highly competitive, but not only will it help you work out if a career at the Bar is the right one for you, it will also demonstrate to prospective chambers that you have done your research, that your interest is longstanding and therefore reliable, and that you are enthusiastic and committed. On the flip side, if you have done little by way of work experience, a chambers is unlikely to take you seriously (nor, for example, might the Inns if and when you apply for a scholarship).

Mini-Pupillage

The most common form of work experience for prospective barristers is the "mini-pupillage". This is an official placement with chambers, usually applied for through a formal process detailed on the chambers website.

Mini-pupillages can last for one day, or may be scheduled to last up to a week. They may be assessed or unassessed. They can be funded or unfunded; and some chambers may reimburse travel expenses.

Typically, a mini-pupil will arrive in chambers and be designated a mini-pupil supervisor. This will be a barrister who has agreed to look after the mini-pupil for the day(s) in question. The mini-pupil will accompany the barrister on his/her daily activities. That may mean the mini-pupil will sit with the barrister in the office, as he/she reads papers or drafts documents, or (if circumstances permit) the barrister may take the mini-pupil along to court with him/her.

It is rarely possible to plan in advance the type of work the mini-pupil will see. That is a natural consequence of the barrister's own schedule, which can change frequently as new work comes in or deadlines are juggled.

In spite of this, barristers will usually aim to give the mini-pupil a flavour of the type of work they carry out, and their general working life in chambers.

Certain mini-pupillages are assessed. You will usually be notified of this in advance. Assessment may be as a formal and official part of the main pupillage application process, or it may simply be in order to have a little additional insight into the abilities of the mini-pupil if he/she was ever to apply for pupillage in future. Whilst they can be daunting, assessed mini-pupillages can be treated as an opportunity to immerse yourself in the typical work of a chambers. It can be as much a useful tool for the mini-pupil to gain a better insight into chambers as it is for the chambers to gain an insight into the mini-pupil. It can also be an excellent way to demonstrate your skills in a real, practical way, which is difficult to achieve by means of a paper application alone.

Full details concerning the mini-pupillage process can usually be found on the chambers website. They are competitive and you are likely to be up against a number of other applicants for a limited number of mini-pupillages offered. Thoroughly check the chambers website for any published selection criteria or application requirements, and comply down to the last letter. They may have a bespoke application form to fill in. If they simply require a

CV and covering letter, set out in your (maximum one-page) covering letter what stage you are at, why you are seeking a mini-pupillage at that particular set, what areas of law interest you (make sure they are areas actually practised by barristers at that chambers!), and then set out why you think you are an ideal candidate for a mini-pupillage. Do not list everything on your CV, but highlight key aspects of your educational and extra-curricular achievements. Finally, if your letter is addressed to a named individual, sign off 'Yours sincerely', whilst it should be 'Yours faithfully' if addressed to 'Sir/Madam'.

Mini-pupillages serve a number of useful functions for the mini-pupil: First to see what the practical reality of working in a particular specialism is like; second to see the kind of work barristers will get at different levels of seniority; third to see the quality of work the chambers in question attracts; fourth to discover the atmosphere and work ethic at the particular chambers; and, separately, to demonstrate your intellect and capabilities to those with whom you are placed.

A few points of caution: The Bar is a small world and when you come to practise you might well come across the same barristers with whom you sat on mini-pupillage. The impression they will have of you is the impression you left them with during your mini-pupillage. It also goes without saying that if you are taken to Court, or meet clients in conference with your supervising barrister, save any questions you may have for the barrister until back in chambers, and do not offer your own opinion to the clients or speak in the conference unless specifically asked to do so.

Once your mini-pupillage is over, make a full note of what you saw, did and learned. This will be useful for pupillage applications. A brief email or card thanking your barrister host is also appreciated.

Vacation Schemes

Law firms have their own formal work experience processes. These often take the form of 'vacation schemes', in which a prospective employee will spend a number of weeks on a placement with the firm, working in one or multiple departments on relatively low-difficulty tasks.

These are often paid – particularly at the commercial London firms – and can be illuminating and invaluable, both for prospective solicitors and also for prospective barristers.

First, it is likely to help you come to a decision in the first place as to whether being a solicitor or barrister is right for you or, indeed, to reaffirm to you that you have made the right choice.

Second, pupillage interviewers love to ask why applicants are opting for a career at the Bar rather than as a solicitor. If you have done work experience with both, you will be in a far better-informed position to answer that question from personal experience.

An additional benefit is the connections you will make. You will have made a number of good friends whilst doing a law degree or the GDL/CPE, who will themselves go on to have impressive legal careers. But every opportunity to make new friends in legal circles at an early stage is an opportunity to build your network for the future.

As before, the application process for work experience with solicitors' firms will usually be detailed on their website. If it is not, you could make contact with their HR or marketing department to explore the options.

If you are not yet at university (and therefore unlikely to meet the requirements to attend a vacation scheme), you should nevertheless approach local firms of solicitors for work experience. You may find yourself photocopying, making coffee or sorting papers, but you will be able to get a feel for the environment and manner of working and will be building important CV points.

Marshalling

Marshalling is the process of undertaking work experience with a member of the judiciary.

Work experience with a judge is particularly useful for those working at the Bar, or hoping to do so, for the obvious reasons that it is the judge who decides the outcome of a case. Judges see different styles of advocacy all the time. It is therefore illuminating to get a feel for how a judge thinks, approaches a case, and views the different styles of advocacy directed towards them. By hearing from the Judge as to what he/she considers makes a good advocate, your own style should improve. Marshalling will also give you further opportunities to see for yourself the advocacy work carried out by barristers

If you intend to practise in a specialist area of law, there is also a high chance that you will regularly appear before judges designated to cases concerning that specialist area of law. Work experience with those judges can enable them to get to know you and to trust you. It can also enable you to understand how they think and work, what irritates them, and what they wish to happen in their courtroom.

The Inns of Court have their own schemes by which they seek to connect prospective barristers with a judge for work experience and, once you have joined an Inn, you can investigate the opportunities on offer through them.

Judges can also be contacted directly, through their clerks. If this is your proposed route, you should send a brief covering letter, politely explaining your current status, that you would appreciate the opportunity for a short period of marshalling, and why you would find this beneficial. You should also include a copy of your CV, together with a stamped, addressed envelope to make a response as easy as possible.

Other Placements

Whilst those placements detailed above represent the most usual 'legal' placements, do not restrict yourself to them if other opportunities present themselves. Thus, for those considering working in shipping law, placements with shipping companies could provide a unique insight into working practices or transactions which might be useful later in understanding the principles or factual scenarios giving rise to legal disputes. Likewise, work experience with an insurance company – getting to know the underwriting process or the relationships with brokers – may be informative for those interested in insurance law. In most areas of law, you will be able to identify a related organisation with 'industry' or 'client' knowledge.

Depending on your specific interests, you should keep a wider eye on this type of work experience, which may reaffirm your proposed specialism, and may also give you the edge on the application forms. They are also likely to give you something a little different to talk about at interviews.

Chapter 9: Other beneficial activities

You will be expected to be proactive in building a CV that showcases your ability to undertake all the tasks expected of a barrister.

The types of characteristic you will need to display are considered in greater detail in Chapter 12 (The Application Process).

Activities to showcase your abilities are, with a little time, effort and dedication, readily available.

You should also set aside time for activities and hobbies you enjoy. Pupillage committees will be looking for rounded individuals with some life experience away from the library, and will also want to take into chambers people they are likely to get along with. It is also very important, for your own well-being, to maintain a work-life balance. Don't abandon your outside interests.

Public Speaking

One of the principal roles of the barrister is that of an advocate. You must be able to speak comfortably, confidently and persuasively. Seize any opportunity available to you to develop this ability.

✓ Join school and university debating societies. If one does not yet exist at school, set it up (thereby showing initiative and motivation at the same time!). At university there will almost invariably be a debating society or grouping, and there are regular national and international competitions which can be entered.

✓ Mooting is also an excellent opportunity to pick up skills required of barristers. Mooting takes the form of a short mock trial focussing on tricky questions of legal principle, given to participants in advance. It usually consists of two teams (A and B) each with two 'barristers', and you may be required to submit a 'skeleton argument' before the advocacy begins, with brief details of your position. Barrister A1 will argue her case on point 1, and barrister B1 will respond. Barrister A2 will then argue his case on point 2 and barrister B2 will respond. The Judges may or may not give permission to respond. They will then give a brief appraisal of the performances and declare a winner. It is not usually something carried out by schools, and you are therefore unlikely to be able to participate in mooting until university. Once at university and law school, a number of opportunities will be available. Some moots will be 'speed moots', prepared under timed conditions; some will require advance preparation; and they will be on different areas of law.

- ✓ Amateur acting or role play is also an activity undertaken by many prospective barristers. You are forced to shed your inhibitions and become used to speaking to an audience. Developing control over the use of your voice is an important skill, too, in the art of persuasion. There will probably be drama clubs at school and in your locality, and certainly at university. Again, where there is a gap, start your own.

- ✓ You may also find media opportunities available to you: university radio or social media can likewise develop public speaking skills. Just be cautious and avoid creating permanent records which you may subsequently come to regret.

Inter-personal Skills

In whichever discipline you choose to practise, you will be required to deal professionally and confidently with judges, clients, witnesses and members of the public. You should therefore develop your interpersonal skills from an early stage.

- ✓ Sign up to charitable activities and voluntary work. This will expose you to a broad spectrum of people. It can range from acting as a cashier at a local charity shop to volunteering at an orphanage on a year abroad or assisting at a retirement home.

✓ Apply for positions on committees to develop your team-work abilities. Obvious choices could be the treasurer of your university law or debating society or charities with a legal element.

Written Skills

A barrister's principal tools are his/her words, written as well as oral. You will be required to draft 'Advices', court documents, opening and closing submissions to a case, skeleton arguments, witness statements and many other documents. Your written skills, therefore, will be something particularly scrutinised by any chambers to which you apply.

✓ Join your school or college magazine. Seek the position of editor if possible.

✓ Contribute to student publications, admissions guides, university fair brochures.

✓ Submit articles to journals and enter essay and legal writing competitions.

Integrity

Possibly the most important requirement for success at the Bar is honesty and integrity. A reputation for sharp or underhand practices can be disastrous for a barrister. It is vital that you are trusted by the Court, which will take at face value much of what you submit; by your clients, who place their faith in you and your advice; by your colleagues, who may seek to discuss their own matters with you on a confidential basis; and by your opponents, who will also trust in your integrity and independence notwithstanding the opposing interests of your clients.

Chambers will therefore wish to see evidence of your honesty and integrity.

✓ Positions in which trust has been placed in you are useful in this regard. You might seek to act as treasurer for a society, or assume a role in which confidential information is entrusted to you.

Pro Bono

From the earliest days of vocational training for the Bar, an emphasis is placed on 'pro bono' work. The Free Representation Unit (FRU) is an excellent example, in which students can work for those without legal representation whilst developing their own skills.[37] Likewise, volunteering for the Citizens' Advice Bureau or legal advice centres can be a fulfilling route to helping those in need of assistance whilst also building your skills and your CV at the same time.

---

[37] The FRU is over-subscribed, so you should sign up early once you have begun the BPTC in order to participate.

Law Fairs

Various universities, training providers and other organisations hold law fairs and pupillage fairs throughout the year.

By way of example, the 2016 Bar Council Pupillage Fair was held at the University of Law in October; the 2016 TARGET Jobs National Pupillage Fair was held in Gray's Inn in November; and the Law Society likewise hosted a London Law Fair in November. These fairs are usually annual, and you will be able to find out more information in respect of future events online.

Carry out research in the legal press and online to ascertain what law and pupillage fairs are being held near you. If there are none near to where you live or study, you may find it useful to sign up to events in London.

Chapter 10: Which area of law?

The first glimpse most of us have into the legal system is the world of criminal law (as seen through the eyes of television script writers). If not *Silk*, *Kavanagh QC*, *Judge John Deed* or *Rumpole of the Bailey*, you will no doubt have seen some other television programmes painting a similarly exciting or glamorous picture of life at the Bar.

A brief trip to your local crown or magistrates' court, to sit in on some of the trials, will soon disrobe you of any idea that it is all gripping theatre. But there is no doubt that crime remains one of the more personal and the more lively areas, the immediacy of its impact being unavoidably apparent and requiring a mastery of both forensic and emotive advocacy unsurpassed by other areas.

There is less scope for entertaining television in respect of other areas. It would be difficult, for example, to attract audiences to a programme concerning the intricacies and legal repercussions of corporate restructuring for tax 'efficiency' savings, or the finer details of a contract dispute between a private school and a tailor over the failure to comply precisely with the contract specification when designing and manufacturing school blazers.

The upshot is that few people, prior to undertaking study in law, have any realistic understanding of the various options available and the realities of a career in the different specialisms.

If you have not had the option of studying Law at A-Level, the first substantive introduction you may get is during your law degree, or on the GDL. But, given the financial and time commitments these require, you would be either brave or foolhardy to enrol on such a course without having at least a basic understanding of the options available and what life in that branch of the profession might entail.

Possibilities within the Bar

Since almost every aspect of life is in some way regulated by the law, and the work of barristers can therefore touch on most aspects of life, the categories of possible specialisation are many and varied. Many overlap and some go by different names depending on whom you ask.[38]

You will find most of the key specialisms reflected in the syllabuses of law degrees in well-reputed universities in England and Wales.[39] However, there are others, some of which are only covered in summary form in university courses, and some of which are not covered at all.

One form of categorisation is that done by the Bar Mutual Indemnity Fund, the Professional Indemnity Insurer for

---

[38] "Employment Law" and "Labour Law" being one such example.
[39] The Law of Scotland differing, in some respects substantially, from that of England and Wales.

barristers, in order to determine what premiums barristers should pay for their professional insurance (the cost of premium varying depending on practice area). Their classification is set out in their 'Ratings Schedule', publicly available on the Bar Mutual website.

Other (perhaps more helpful, though by no means exclusive) categorisations are those set out by the various rankings agencies, which publish public rankings of barristers and chambers to enable clients and solicitors to find and instruct the 'top' barristers in a given area. One such example is Chambers & Partners, which currently ranks the UK Bar in the following categories:

- Administrative & Public Law
- Agriculture & Rural Affairs
- Art & Cultural Property Law
- Aviation
- Banking & Finance
- Chancery
- Chancery: Commercial
- Chancery: Traditional
- Charities
- Civil Liberties & Human Rights
- Clinical Negligence
- Commercial Dispute Resolution
- Community Care
- Company
- Competition Law
- Construction
- Consumer Law
- Costs Litigation

- Court of Protection: Health & Welfare
- Court of Protection: Property & Affairs
- Crime
- Crime: International Criminal Law
- Data Protection
- Defamation/Privacy
- Education
- Election Law
- Employment
- Energy & Natural Resources
- Environment
- European Law
- Extradition
- Family/Matrimonial
- Family: Children
- Family: Matrimonial Finance
- Financial Crime
- Financial Crime: Corporates
- Financial Services
- Fraud: Civil
- Health & Safety
- Immigration
- Information Technology
- Inquests & Public Inquiries
- Insurance
- Intellectual Property
- International Arbitration: Arbitrators
- International Arbitration: Construction/Engineering
- International Arbitration: General Commercial & Insurance

- Licensing
- Local Government
- Media & Entertainment
- Media Law
- Mediators
- Motor Insurance Fraud
- Offshore
- Partnership
- Pensions
- Personal Injury
- Personal Injury: Industrial Disease
- Planning
- Planning & Environment
- Proceeds of Crime Act Work & Asset Forfeiture
- Police Law: Mainly Claimant
- Police Law: Mainly Defendant
- Product Liability
- Professional Discipline
- Professional Negligence
- Professional Negligence: Technology & Construction
- Property Damage
- Public International Law
- Public Procurement
- Real Estate Litigation
- Restructuring/Insolvency
- Sanctions
- Shipping & Commodities
- Social Housing
- Sport
- Tax

- Tax: Indirect Tax
- Tax: Private Client
- Telecommunications
- Travel: International Personal Injury
- Travel: Regulatory & Commercial
- Trusts

The above list is extensive, and demonstrates the breadth of possibilities available at the Bar. However, not all within the list are, of themselves, sufficient to maintain a full practice: there will be insufficient work in some areas to sustain a practice on its own, and some are so niche that a broader knowledge would be required in any event to provide comprehensive legal advice to your client. Conversely, some 'common law' practitioners will leave their practice very much open and will carry out a wide spectrum of work covering many of the areas identified above.

How to Choose

Do not feel overwhelmed by the choices available. Whilst the above list of areas is extensive, their overlapping nature means that they are often grouped together both in academic courses and also by sets of chambers.

There are a number of stages through which you will go on your route towards pupillage, during which you will sample different areas of law.

Thus, you will have to complete the seven core foundation subjects (Public Law, which includes Constitutional Law, Administrative Law and Human Rights; EU Law; Criminal

Law; Contract; Tort and Restitution; Property/Land Law; and Equity and the Law of Trusts). These cover the broadest principles of most areas of law.

You may also have the option to undertake further modules, such as Media, Tax, Employment, and Family, particularly if your exploration is in the course of an undergraduate degree. When it comes to selecting which modules to undertake, you should thoroughly examine the syllabuses to determine whether the subject area interests you academically and intellectually. This will give a solid basis for determining whether or not it will interest you in practice, since much of law revolves around research, application and advice on questions of law – actions not dissimilar to the work of a barrister in practice.

Many people find a natural inclination for certain areas as they undertake their degree or GDL. You may also have certain wishes in relation to:

➢ a desired level of court-based advocacy
➢ a desired level of written work in chambers
➢ an ability to work from home
➢ income levels
➢ a preferred variety in legal or factual scenarios
➢ a wish to work with and for private individuals
➢ a desire to do social good in your work
➢ a preference for international work and travel
➢ the pace at which an area of law develops and is subject to influence by your work
➢ the type of client you wish to work for

If you have a previous career in a particular sector, you may also wish to utilise the skills or knowledge you have built up and could bring to bear.

There is also a wide variety of reading material available to you when looking at different practice areas. The textbooks and practitioner works, of which you will become aware during your university tuition, are good places to start. Otherwise, go out and purchase text books independently, or visit legal libraries where they are available for your use. Don't forget, for example, that the libraries of the Inns of Court will be available to you as a student once you are a member. You can also access High Court and Court of Appeal judgments on the website www.bailii.org by following the link to England and Wales Case Law and selecting your preferred area of interest.[40]

Finally, in order to see the practical reality of work in the areas you have selected, apply for work experience and lots of it. Use this as an opportunity to ask about the area of law, its pros and cons, and the amount of advocacy involved, compared to written work. Ask about the type of clients, the working hours, whether instructions come in at the last minute, the stresses and pressures of the job. Ask about its suitability for your own goals or preferences, whatever they may be. Whilst most barristers will be reluctant to disclose the amount they are earning to a work experience student, you can also try asking, in general terms, about the relative

---

[40] The categorisation on Bailii is once again different, albeit relatively self-explanatory. The Court of Appeal judgments are separated into Criminal cases and Civil (non-criminal) cases; whilst the High Court judgments are split out into more specific groupings dependent on the court in which they were heard.

remuneration of the area as against other areas – albeit ensuring that you ask this question only when and to whom you perceive it appropriate.

Practice Development

For some, the area of law which first attracted them to the Bar will be the area in which they subsequently come to specialise. For most, however, it will form merely the first taste of the wider banquet of areas available.

The menu is large and there is no rush to decide. Indeed, the careers of some at the Bar will change markedly over time, moving from one practice area to another. This could be for any number of reasons: a reduction in available work in one area; more attractive fees in others; dislike of the area or the working conditions; or even sheer luck in taking on one case in a different area, which leads to a proliferation of similar instructions...

For the most part, however, the area in which you commence practice will define or, at the very least, influence the remainder of your career. It is, therefore, important to give thorough consideration to the question of which area or areas of law you wish to focus on or specialise in.

In the end, your practice can be as broad or as narrow as your interest takes you. Some will place themselves under the broad umbrella of 'commercial law', which encompasses most disputes relating to companies, trade and commerce. Some will focus more particularly on IT and telecoms disputes, or insurance disputes, each of which loosely fall within the description 'commercial law', but which have their own specific bodies of law. Some might practise generally in family law, whilst some will limit themselves to work relating to children. Some might practise generally in crime, whilst some will do only prosecution or defence work.

That said, in reality, most barristers will at least begin life at the Bar practising in a broad field before, over the years and as their practice develops, finding themselves becoming more and more specialist in one particular part of that field.

You will have to find a balance in your practice development between (a) narrowing, to specialise (which allows you to become an expert in a particular area, gaining expertise and advantage over your opponents, and leading to the most interesting and high-profile work of that type, and thus the highest fees) and (b) keeping your options open (which can bring a greater diversity of work, can enable you to transfer learning or principles from one area to shed light on another, can mean more readily available work, and can be safer if the legal disputes in one narrow specialism reduce for a period of time due to wider political, economic or legal reasons, but can conversely lead to a reduced level of knowledge in specialist areas).

You will also have to monitor the speed and time at which you narrow your specialism: some who gain pupillage at specialist sets will, from the outset, practise in a very narrow field; others, who are taken on by a chambers practising more broadly, will have opportunities in a number of fields and will have to decide when, and the extent to which, they wish to focus on one area to the exclusion of others.

These, however, are questions you will keep under review for a number of years. They are something you will come to decide, in consultation with your clerks, as your career develops. For the moment, simply keep in mind that your choice of area of law will shape and influence the rest of your career, though there will, in all likelihood, remain a certain degree of flexibility for you to direct your own path.

For those studying law as an undergraduate degree, aim to get a broad idea of the areas of interest to you in the first couple of years of university and, at the same time, undertake work experience in those areas to confirm your feelings. Then, as you undertake optional modules, select those modules which would assist in those areas of interest.

For those pursuing other paths, aim to adopt a similar strategy over the years before pupillage applications. You may find it slightly more difficult, since you will not be reading law day in day out, but take the initiative: carry out independent study, visit libraries, purchase legal text books, speak with your contemporaries who are reading law, attend public court hearings, read some recent judgments from sources such as 'Bailii' (detailed above) and apply for work experience.

Chapter 11: Selecting the perfect Chambers

Once you have determined that you wish to pursue a career at the Bar, and you have an idea of the general areas in which you wish to practise, it is time to begin narrowing your focus to particular chambers. When there are so many, the task can feel particularly daunting. The best way to approach the question is through a methodical series of steps, dependent upon what you consider to be important in your career.

Specialism

The first and most obvious stage in filtering down the chambers is by specialism.

Some chambers will specialise in one area alone; others will specialise in multiple areas. You should consider whether you wish to focus immediately on one particular area of law, which might for example suit someone who has had a previous career in industry in that field or who is certain about their interest, or whether you wish to practise more broadly and keep your options open for specialism later down the line.

To ascertain the best chambers in your chosen specialism(s), begin with the pupillage guides, such as the Training Contract & Pupillage Handbook, and the directories of rankings such as Chambers & Partners and Legal 500.

You can also see in the reports of cases[41] which barristers acted for the parties. Identify recent major cases in areas of interest and carry out internet searches on the named barristers to find out the chambers in which they practise.

Location

You may have a particular desire to work in a certain location, whether for personal reasons (perhaps a particular city where your family or partner resides) or career reasons (perhaps due to the concentration of high quality work in a particular region).

This is perfectly possible in specialisms such as crime or employment, which have opportunities for high quality work in cities and the 'provinces' across the country. You can carry out a quick test by conducting a search on the internet for chambers specialising in your desired area in

---

[41] If you have started legal training, you will probably have access to these reports on electronic platforms such as Westlaw and LexisNexis. Otherwise, they can be accessed by anybody through www.bailii.org

your desired location to see if there is sufficient work there to justify a set of chambers specialising in that discipline.

With some other specialisms, there is a lot less flexibility in location if you wish to obtain the better work. Many have a particular London focus, with the most highly-ranked specialist chambers grouped within a fairly tight radius around Temple, Holborn and Chancery Lane. Likewise, specialist branches of the High Court such as the Technology and Construction Court, Commercial Court and Intellectual Property Enterprise Court are based in central London. Even in respect of the bigger cases held at trial centres around the country, counsel from London will frequently be instructed rather than local counsel.

It should also be borne in mind that the work of a barrister will frequently involve large amounts of travel, as a result of which it can sometimes be impossible to be permanently ensconced in one location.

Atmosphere

An important but often underestimated factor in choosing a chambers is the atmosphere. Not all chambers are the same. On the contrary, they can vary wildly dependent on the personalities of their members and clerks, and their work ethic. Some chambers have developed a strong focus on 'commerciality', or on reflecting the friendly and practical approach of their clients; others are more formal and take a more traditional approach.

Your chambers will play an important role in your development, both in how you manage the stresses and workload of the job and, also, in the types of clients you get (with their varying attitudes) and how you interact with them. It is therefore important that you work somewhere which provides you with the right level of support and with an atmosphere in which you feel comfortable. What might suit one person might be utterly inappropriate for another.

Judging the atmosphere of a chambers is almost impossible without attending work experience there or meeting barristers at the set yourself. Websites can sometimes give a diluted 'feel' of the set's approach, but bear in mind that they are principally written as marketing material and might therefore present a glossy and unrealistic picture. You may also be able to meet some of the barristers during pupillage fairs, or at educational or outreach events staged by chambers, universities or the Inns of Court.

Quality and quantity of work

Although you are self-employed and the work you attract will hinge partly on your own personal reputation, at least in the first few years a considerable quantity of work will also come through to you based solely or largely on the reputation of your chambers. Thus, if you are a member of a highly-ranked or well-known chambers, it is likely that there will be a regular flow of high quality work which will be funnelled to you by the clerks. If, on the other hand, your chambers has not yet established a reputation (or, even worse, is not well thought of), it is likely that you will not be busy, and certainly not with high quality work.

To identify the more reputable chambers, trawl the various directories available, such as www.legal500.com and Chambers & Partners. The exercise discussed above, of identifying recent judgments of interest and locating the chambers at which the barristers in the case are members, can also be a useful starting point.

Chapter 12: The Application Process

As you ought to know by now, self-employed barristers in chambers are simply individuals who work together in the development of a collective reputation and to benefit from shared premises and resources. A barrister's reputation and work stream is, therefore, intimately connected with the work and reputation of the other barristers in chambers.

This means that the pupillage and tenancy process is an important one, not only for the applicants, but also for the existing barristers in chambers. If an inappropriate person is accepted, there can be wider ramifications on the other members of chambers. Your reputation will affect theirs and vice versa. So it is natural that they will want the best applicants; the applicants who will reflect best on them and their chambers; who show an interest in the type of work typically carried out by their chambers; who demonstrate strong academic ability and who will impress solicitors so that work will keep coming in.

The Application Procedure

Different chambers apply different procedures in their pupillage process. Your first port of call should always be the individual chambers' website. This will often set out the various stages in their assessment process so that you know what to expect.

Many chambers use the Bar Council's online Pupillage Gateway to begin their application procedure.[42] Vacancies are advertised on the Gateway, and the applications for a large number of chambers are submitted through it. Other chambers adopt their own, bespoke application procedures which they will detail separately.

Applicants are able to submit up to a total of 12 applications through the Gateway, using the online application form. There is a 'submissions window', which is the period of time during which applications can be submitted. This lasts for one month, and it is not possible to submit applications after this time. The status of the applications can then be tracked online.

In 2017, the submissions window lasted from 9 January to 7 February. First and second round interview offers were sent out between February and April, and offers of pupillage were made from 3 May. These dates fell some 3 months earlier than the same stages 2016, so it is imperative that you make reference to the website well in advance to avoid missing any deadlines.

---

[42] See http://www.pupillagegateway.com

Chambers which do not use the Gateway tend to operate the same, or a similar, process: a written application form (or CV plus covering letter); one or two rounds of interview; and sometimes a written or oral assessment.

Applicants will tend to find that the non-Gateway chambers have deadlines beginning earlier than the Gateway deadline. By bringing their application process forward in this way, chambers seek to snap up the best candidates early on. You should carefully consider potential chambers well in advance of the Gateway season, and watch out for non-Gateway application processes and deadlines, in order not to miss potential applications for some excellent chambers. Applications take an extraordinary length of time to complete if done properly: you will probably have strict word limits and will spend hours trimming a sentence here or there, or alighting upon the perfect phraseology; and identifying the right examples to illustrate the skills required is likely to take longer than you would at first think. Avoid typographical errors at all costs: these can be immediately fatal to applications.

It is also worthwhile bearing in mind that, whilst there are a maximum 12 applications which can be made through the Gateway, there are no restrictions on the number of pupillages a candidate can apply for outside the Gateway. By increasing the number of applications you submit, you are increasing your chances of success.

Proof-read your applications again and again; ask friends, family, professors and anyone else you can recruit to read them and give their opinions.

The Assessment Criteria

Whilst chambers will have their own ways of formulating the criteria against which you will be tested, they are usually aiming at the same target.

The assessment criteria are often expressly detailed in the Pupillage section of the set's website, but even where they are not detailed, you should aim to showcase a similar portfolio of skills in application forms, interviews and written assessments you may be given.

Typically, you will be expected to demonstrate the following types of skill and ability:

> ➤ Academic achievement and intellectual ability. This will usually be through examination results at school, university and law school; awards and prizes received and membership of clubs or societies which demonstrate high intellectual abilities.

> ➤ Analytical skills. As a barrister, you will need to absorb complex factual and expert information and analyse its application to the law. You should expect to be able to demonstrate your skills in this area through previous academic and extra-curricular activities.

> ➤ Advocacy. The need for these skills goes without saying. Strong candidates will have undertaken debating and mooting at university, or will have evidence of other examples of public speaking and oral presentation skills.

➢ Written skills. This will be more important in certain disciplines than others. In commercial chambers, for example, written skills are of high importance. Your application form itself will, in part, be a test of your written skills, and you should ensure that any covering letter and any text within the application form is clear, concise and grammatically correct. Other examples of written skills (such as editing magazines, publishing articles) will also be valuable.

➢ Determination. A career at the bar requires a lot of self-motivation and drive. You will be expected to demonstrate your commitment to the career. Work experience and a thorough understanding of the demands of life at the Bar can assist in this regard.

➢ Independence. The Bar is a solitary environment where your work is your own, and you will rarely have anyone to supervise or approve it. You will need to exhaust all options for legal research when advising your clients and take the initiative in finding and formulating arguments. Chambers will expect you to demonstrate an ability to work independently and to deal with pressure and stressful situations.

➢ Interpersonal skills. Few professions will lead to contact with as diverse an array of clients as those found at the Bar. You will be expected to deal with Judges one moment and difficult, potentially criminal, clients the next. You should also be able to build strong working relationships with other barristers and with legal and lay clients. Assessors will expect you to have examples of your ability to demonstrate a solid track record of interpersonal skills.

➤ Integrity. Your reputation at the Bar is built on integrity. It is a requirement of your code of conduct, but it also has real practical implications when dealing with judges, opponents and clients. Your actions reflect on your chambers and you will be expected to act with integrity at all times. Your assessor will be looking for evidence of this. Roles such as treasurer in societies, or occasions when you have acted with honesty, will be useful in this regard.

Where chambers' websites specifically set out the criteria they will be applying, you would be well-advised to address each element separately in their application forms (space permitting). This will enable the assessors, in the early rounds, to see clearly that you have achieved their requirements, and should assist in getting your application placed on the 'Invite to Interview' pile.

Referees

You are likely to be asked for references at the time of your application. Give some thought to this long before the application deadline, as you will need to get permission from your referees in advance. You may also wish to discuss your application and career goals with them and answer any questions they may have. Once you submit your application, provide them with a copy of your CV and application form, to ensure that they are aware of your relevant qualifications and extra-curricular activities.

You will probably be asked for two references. At least one should be an academic reference, usually from a university or law school tutor. It goes without saying that your requested referee should be someone you trust, and who has enough faith in and knowledge of your abilities to give you a positive and credible reference. If you are asked for a personal referee, opt for a professional if possible.

Keep your referee informed as the process progresses, and remind them of any applicable deadlines as they approach: your reference is unlikely to be uppermost in their minds or list of priorities.

The Interview

Chambers may have one or more rounds of interview. They may inform you in advance of the nature and content of the interview, or they may not. In any event, you should always expect the unexpected and prepare well.

A first round interview may consist of an informal discussion with one or a small number of members of chambers. It may be intended to probe the honesty or accuracy of your application form, or to find out further details. Equally, it may be a more in-depth, legal interview, requiring you to have prepared answers to a problem question or to analyse scenarios on the spot.

A second round interview is likely to be more demanding. The number of potential pupils will have been narrowed further, and you can expect to be questioned in detail about your past experience, your views on the Bar in general and on the chambers in particular, and your interest in the areas of law in which the set specialises.

It should go without saying that you should be familiar with the main specialisms of the chambers to which you are applying. You would also be well-advised to have topics prepared for discussion on:

> ➤ Why you want to be a barrister (and why you do not wish instead to be a solicitor).

> ➤ Why you are interested in the law and, specifically, the areas in which chambers specialises.

> ➤ Why you have applied to the chambers in question. Mini-pupillages are an excellent method of proving genuine interest in, and commitment to, the chambers. Likewise, the set's ranking in the bar directories might have been a factor in your interest.

> ➤ Recent published cases by members of chambers. These can usually be found by looking at 'News' sections of the chambers

website, or by looking at individual barristers' profiles (which will often set out cases in which they have been involved).

➤ Recent legal developments which you have found to be of interest. These might include significant recent legal decisions in areas relevant to chambers or procedural changes in the legal system generally. There have, of course, been many such procedural changes in recent years, including the changes to cost budgeting (following the Jackson review) which have had a major impact; changes to legal aid; the Quality Assurance Scheme for Advocacy relating to the assessment of criminal advocates. There are likely to be further changes (Lord Justice Briggs has recently conducted a review of the organisation of the Courts[43], and Lord Justice Jackson has given a supplemental report on fixed recoverable costs[44]).

➤ Recent political or current affairs-related questions. Keep abreast of the news and aim to have reasoned positions on the major issues of the day. Aim to be articulate and balanced, and steer clear of expressing too extreme a political

---

[43] See https://www.judiciary.gov.uk/civil-courts-structure-review/civil-courts-structure-review-ccsr-final-report-published
[44] See https://www.judiciary.gov.uk/publications/review-of-civil-litigation-costs-supplemental-report-fixed-recoverable-costs/

viewpoint if you wish to avoid alienating members of the interview panel.

➤ Yourself. Chambers will want to know more about your interests, hobbies and achievements. They will want to know that you are someone who would fit in and that they could happily work alongside you for the next 30 years. Be neither pompous nor 'matey', but pitch yourself as friendly but professional.

You should also re-read your application. It should be as fresh in your mind as it is in the minds of the pupillage panel (who will have it to hand), as they are likely to probe into the matters you have set out or expressed an interest in.

You should think carefully about your appearance for interviews. Pitch it at the right level for the set in question (this is another consideration where you would benefit from having spent some time at the chambers on mini-pupillage). You should always dress smartly: a dark trouser/skirt suit is usual and unobjectionable. There are some sets which are very informal, and where a little accessorising would be nothing more than a distinctive talking point. At others, however, some red shoes or a fluorescent tie may spell the end of your application. Where in any doubt at all, err on the side of caution.

Ensure your body language is professional and confident. If you shake hands with one assessor, shake hands with them all. Maintain good eye contact, and answer questions directly. Breathe slowly, talk slowly, think quickly.

If you are not used to interviews, or have had little experience, try to obtain some interview practice. There are certain companies which offer mock interviews; or seek an interview from a professional friend, Inn mentor / sponsor or family member. You may also be able to persuade your university tutor or a teacher to offer a mock interview. Law schools often also offer mock interviews. You would be well-advised to take every opportunity you can.

Finally, try recording yourself on your phone responding to practice questions in advance, in order to listen to, assess and improve on your speaking style. Are you speaking slowly and clearly? Do you sound like you believe what you are saying, or are you hesitant and uncertain? Is your answer sensible and does it answer the question?

Applications outside the norm

If for some reason you are in an unusual situation, or a situation in which you would wish for additional guidance in respect of a specific application process, there would be nothing stopping you from contacting the chambers in question well in advance to make enquiries.

You may wish to ask about their specific criteria or how, in your situation, you might fulfil them.

Equally, you may find benefit in attending a mini-pupillage and discussing this with your mini-pupil supervisor, or (if possible) a member of the chambers' pupillage committee.

Chapter 13: CVs

Your CV is not only important for *what* it says but also for *how* it says it. It is the first glimpse the assessor has into your personality; your ability to organise and prioritise; what you think is important; and how you are able to present yourself. These are important skills in themselves, particularly for a career at the Bar. If your CV is a mess, that is the impression you give of yourself.

You should, therefore, spend plenty of time on your CV. It goes without saying that any foolish typographical errors will undermine your application. Check carefully for these. There are also some other basic principles you should bear in mind:

- ✓ Pick a sensible font. You cannot go wrong with Times New Roman.
- ✓ Set out the CV in clearly headed sections.
- ✓ Begin with your name, date of birth and contact details. Use an appropriate email address. You may find mad_madge@sillysausage.com amusing. The assessor will not.

- ✓ Set out your education, work experience, scholarships/awards, relevant roles you have had, public speaking and advocacy, and other interests.
- ✓ Arrange your sections in reverse-chronological order, most recent achievements first.
- ✓ Keep it to bullet points or short sentences. Where there are hundreds of applicants, assessors do not have time to plough through dense paragraphs of text.
- ✓ Obey the two-page rule. Unless you have such a glittering list of achievements that it is impossible to limit yourself to two, your CV should not go over to a third side of A4.

- ✗ Don't write in lengthy paragraphs. Keep it short and to the point.
- ✗ No flashy colours. Remember: smart, subdued and professional. "Eccentric" is not a criterion on most chambers' list of desired traits.
- ✗ Unless specifically requested to do so, it is not usual to include a photo. If a photo is requested, ensure you provide an application-appropriate snap. Clothes and hair should be as you would have them in an interview: smart and neat.
- ✗ If you have a brimming CV, filter out the less impressive. The assessor won't want to hear about your beginner's front crawl swimming certificate.

Two sample CVs are included at Appendix 1 at the end of this book, for illustrative purposes. They are a guide only.

You can include categories of information not set out in the samples if it is information which would improve your application. You should also search for other templates online to get a feel for other ways in which the information can be set out. Ultimately, you should make sure that your CV conveys the image you wish to present of yourself.

Different chambers adopt different procedures for pupillage applicants.[45] Those chambers with application processes outside the Pupillage Gateway may request CVs. Others will have their own application forms. The same principles as described above should be adopted with application forms. They are the first thing the assessor sees and, given the high numbers of applicants, if your form is not clear and organised and does not look professional, your prospects will take an immediate hit.

Now, CV prepared and submitted, picture the scene:

The assessor, probably a barrister on the pupillage committee, sitting in his/her office in chambers, has a large pile of pupillage or mini-pupillage applications sitting on the desk. This person is, no doubt, already overworked with deadlines looming for demanding solicitors, and pressure building from the clerks.

Ask yourself, does your CV stand out among the crowd? And if it does, is it standing out for the right reason? Which pile will it be put in? Your assessor needs to know you have

---

[45] See Chapter 12.

strong academic qualifications, that you are motivated, that you have a track record of interest in the law and that you would be a positive addition to chambers. Make sure this is the message you are conveying by your CV or application form, and ask teachers, trusted friends or family to check it over for you.

Chapter 14: Hot Topics for Interview

Whilst there is unlikely to be space on the pupillage application forms to ask you in detail about your knowledge of recent developments in the law, legal processes or issues, your interviewers are likely to assess your interest in the career by reference to such recent events.

You should therefore ensure that you are fully aware of, and prepared to answer questions on, 'hot topics' relevant to the profession.

You may, for example, be asked to detail *"what development in the law has interested you recently"*, or *"what do you see as the main issues or risks affecting the profession at the moment"*. You may be asked about *"any recent or proposed reforms to Court processes"* or perhaps *"what topical case law or legislation has caught your attention"*.

Whilst these questions may feel somewhat intimidating, they are, in fact, all designed to elicit the same underlying information about you: whether you are genuinely interested in the profession and understand the career you are seeking to join.

With sufficient research and preparation, they can all be answered easily, with topics targeted to the specialism of the set in question.

For example, if asked about new case law by a chambers which is concerned with contract law (including the vast majority of civil sets), you may wish to raise one of the Supreme Court's recent decisions re-defining the law.

Example

The Supreme Court had previously said in an earlier case called *Rainy Sky v Kookmin Bank* [2011] UKSC 50 that, where there are two potential interpretations of a particular clause, the Court should prefer the one which is most consistent with commercial common sense.

More recently, in *Arnold v Britton* [2015] UKSC 36,[46] however, the Supreme Court again considered the general rules for interpretation of Contracts. The 'new' approach was widely considered to have signalled a move away from a more flexible and commercial interpretation to a renewed focus on the precise words used in the contract.

In this regard, Lord Neuberger stated in his Judgment that, *"the reliance placed in some cases on commercial common sense and surrounding circumstances ... should not be invoked to undervalue*

---

[46] Which can be located on www.bailii.org by searching for the name or citation reference ([2015] UKSC 36)

the importance of the language of the provision which is to be construed. The exercise of interpreting a provision involves identifying what the parties meant through the eyes of a reasonable reader, and, save perhaps in a very unusual case, that meaning is most obviously to be gleaned from the language of the provision. Unlike commercial common sense and the surrounding circumstances, the parties have control over the language they use in a contract. And, again save perhaps in a very unusual case, the parties must have been specifically focussing on the issue covered by the provision when agreeing the wording of that provision."

Many practitioners in the commercial sphere considered this to be a worrying development for some clients who frequently enter into contracts quickly without giving detailed consideration to the precise language used, and who may later be tripped up by too technical or literal an interpretation when that would fly in the face of common sense or what the parties had in mind at the time.

The matter came again before the Supreme Court in the recent case of *Wood v Capita Insurance Services Ltd* [2017] UKSC 24.[47] Lord Hodge rejected the notion that *Arnold v Britton* had changed the law, and instead reconciled the two cases. He stated that,

---

[47] Which can be located on www.bailii.org by searching for the name or citation reference ([2017] UKSC 24).

"Interpretation is... a unitary exercise; where there are rival meanings, the court can give weight to the implications of rival constructions by reaching a view as to which construction is more consistent with business common sense. But, in striking a balance between the indications given by the language and the implications of the competing constructions the court must consider the quality of drafting of the clause ...; and it must also be alive to the possibility that one side may have agreed to something which with hindsight did not serve his interest...

"This unitary exercise involves an iterative process by which each suggested interpretation is checked against the provisions of the contract and its commercial consequences are investigated... To my mind once one has read the language in dispute and the relevant parts of the contract that provide its context, it does not matter whether the more detailed analysis commences with the factual background and the implications of rival constructions or a close examination of the relevant language in the contract, so long as the court balances the indications given by each."

There can be little doubt that most practitioners viewed *Arnold v Britton* as a change in approach from that adopted previously; and the reaffirmation by the Supreme Court of the more traditional approach, which has an eye on commerciality, has been broadly welcomed.

Other similar examples include:

> ➢ the Supreme Court's decision in *Marks & Spencer v BNP Paribas Securities Services Trust Co* [2015] UKSC 72, in which the Court reversed the Privy Council's formulation in respect of when terms would be implied into contracts. The Privy Council had previously said in *Attorney General of Belize v Belize Telecom* [2009] that the contract should be construed as a whole to determine whether the reasonable reader would understand the term to have been implied. In *Marks & Spencer*, the Supreme Court did away with this formulation and reimposed the traditional tests of implication only where necessary to give the contract business efficacy or so obvious that it went without saying.

> ➢ the Supreme Court's decision in *Makdessi v Cavendish Square Holdings BV* [2015] UKSC 67 in which the Court considered the historic rules relating to penalty clauses in contracts and if/when they were valid. In this case, whilst it was invited to re-write the rules, it instead confirmed that a term in a contract which constituted a penalty was unenforceable, and that something was a penalty if it was a secondary obligation which imposed a detriment on the contract-breaker out of all proportion to any legitimate interest of the innocent party in the enforcement of the primary obligation.

Equally, if asked about recent developments in legislation, you may wish to draw upon the various changes made by Parliament to UK insurance law recently.

> **Example**
>
> Until recently, due to a line of cases including *Sprung v Royal Assurance (UK) Ltd* [1997] CLC 70, an insured person who suffered further losses (such as losses of profits) as a result of an insurer's failure to pay money due under an insurance policy within a reasonable time, was not entitled to recover those additional losses from the insurer.
>
> This has, for many years, proved highly controversial. The Enterprise Act 2016 inserted into the Insurance Act 2015 a provision requiring insurers to pay valid claims within a reasonable time, and permitting the insured to recover additional losses where the insurer failed to do so.

As to reforms of the Court processes, there have been a number of changes recently, principally brought about by the Jackson Review of Civil Litigation Costs.

> **Example**
>
> One of the changes with the widest impact following the Jackson Review has been the rules in relation to what is known as 'cost budgeting'.

Before the new rules came into effect, the Court did not usually enquire how much parties to litigation were spending on their legal representation until the end of the case, at which point the costs were presented to the Court and the losing party was usually required to pay the majority of the winning party's costs.

It was considered by Lord Justice Jackson that the cost of litigation had come to be excessive and out of proportion, and required active management by the Court during the litigation process. Accordingly, a regime of 'cost budgeting' has been established, by which the parties have to set out their estimated costs in a standard form at the beginning of the legal process and have these costs approved or reduced by the Court. The lawyers may still charge their clients as much as they agree between them, but the consequence of cost budgeting is that, at the end of trial, the costs *recoverable* by the winning party against the losing party will be limited to those set out in their budget.

These reforms are viewed with mixed feelings. Some barristers see them as a success, insofar as clients are now fully apprised of the likely costs of the case through to trial, and it helps in focussing minds on settlement before the costs are incurred. Conversely, the cost budgeting process can itself add to the time spent on preparation or in Court and therefore increase the costs incurred.

In terms of future reforms, there are a number of sources at which you would be well-advised to look.

> The Law Commission carries out research and consultations and makes proposals for legal reform, which can provide fertile ground both for interview topics on areas of potential problems in the current law and also on areas of potential future reform.

> The Briggs Review on the Civil Courts Structure has also been published recently,[48] and the way in which it might be implemented remains to be seen.

> Lord Justice Jackson has given a supplemental report on fixed recoverable costs,[49] with a view to limiting the costs recoverable in certain types of case or for certain values. Again, the way in which this might be implemented remains to be seen.

> Related to crime is the controversial Quality Assurance Scheme for Advocates (QASA), which was challenged and upheld by the Supreme Court on 24 June 2015. It remains to be implemented. It is a scheme in England and Wales, applicable to all advocates whether they are acting for the prosecution or defence, and is intended to assess and assure the quality of criminal advocacy in the courts by reference to

---

[48]   See   https://www.judiciary.gov.uk/civil-courts-structure-review/civil-courts-structure-review-ccsr-final-report-published
[49]   See   https://www.judiciary.gov.uk/publications/review-of-civil-litigation-costs-supplemental-report-fixed-recoverable-costs/

the same set of standards, regardless of an advocate's previous education and training. It led to various fears including over the independence of the barristers. Further information is readily available online.

Rather than being asked open questions, you may, on the other hand, be asked about a specific development selected by the interview panel. It is, therefore, clearly important to read the legal press, such as the Times legal pages,[50] and to keep on top of current events as far as possible.

If you arrive at interview and are asked about a topic of which you are genuinely unaware, resist the temptation to 'wing it' or guess what it may be about, or to try to obfuscate your way through an answer. You are likely to get it wrong and come across as confused or, worse, dishonest. Better to be frank and admit that you are not aware of the particular issue mentioned. You could then ask to what the panel is referring, or seek to steer the topic onto reforms with which you are more familiar.

---

[50] Be wary of reliance on the more light hearted legal sites such as www.rollonfriday.com

Chapter 15: Pupillage

If you are one of the successful few to obtain a pupillage, congratulations! But the hard work is not over yet...

Your pupillage will last 12 months and you will be placed with one or more pupil supervisors (historically known as pupil masters or pupil mistresses). Full details of your pupillage, including the procedure and what is expected of you, should be made known to you in advance. It may be detailed on the chambers website, or set out in an internal policy document. If it is not, have a word with the head of pupillage, or your supervisor, to ascertain the position.

It is then over to you to demonstrate to all those with whom you come into contact that you are intelligent, hard-working and an asset to the chambers.

Pupil Supervisors

In order to be a pupil supervisor, the barrister must have been formally approved by their Inn and will have gone through a briefing. That is the extent of the uniformity, and there is otherwise no 'typical' supervisor about whom you can be forewarned.

You will most likely be sharing your supervisor's office for the duration of your time with him/her. Exercise the common courtesies to be expected in such an environment: Ensure that you are at all times appropriately dressed, that your belongings are tidy, that you are courteous and responsive, and that you carry out the tasks requested of you on time and with a minimum of fuss. Do not distract your supervisor unnecessarily or engage in personal phone calls in the same room. Learn by example and accept constructive criticism (giving the supervisor, who may well be tired, stressed and overworked, the benefit of the doubt that the criticism was intended to be constructive).

Tasks and Assessments

You are likely to be given a number of pieces of work to carry out for your supervisor(s) and for other members of chambers.

It is possible that your performance on any given piece of work will have no impact whatsoever on the ultimate decision of whether or not to grant you tenancy. Conversely, each piece of work you carry out from the outset may be assessed and contribute to the final decision. Try to ascertain how your chambers assessment process works and, if you do not know, assume that everything is assessed. In any event, the opinion of each barrister for whom you work may well be important in the decision-making process.

You may also be given formal assessment tasks. These may take the form of written advices or pleadings, or may be oral advocacy tasks. You may even be required to engage in adversarial advocacy against other pupils in chambers. Whilst stressful, bear in mind that these tasks are designed to enable you to showcase your skills and abilities. You will not be expected at this stage to be a fully-polished and experienced barrister, but you will be expected to carry out all relevant research and to present a reasoned and professional case. Use them as an opportunity to develop your style and demonstrate why you would be an asset to chambers.

Second Six

In your second six months of pupillage, you may also be given the opportunity to go out and exercise rights of audience before the Courts. This will usually take the form of minor application hearings or small claims, where you will be able to practise your written and oral advocacy skills in a relatively low pressure environment.

These are rare opportunities to get out of chambers and exercise a little freedom and independence on your own. Enjoy them, and use them to hone your skills in readiness for the larger cases.

Nevertheless, you should speak with your supervisor or other junior members of chambers in advance of attending Court, or providing the piece of work, if you are unsure of what to do or how a case should be approached. Ensure that you have the phone numbers for the clerks, your supervisor and the Bar Council Ethics Enquiries Service saved to your mobile phone before heading out, in case some urgent assistance is needed.

Additional Training

You must register your pupillage as soon as possible with your Inn and you will be required to undertake further education in parallel with your work in chambers. This additional training is provided by the Inn and includes an advocacy course (usually on a residential weekend away, subsidised by the Inn) and a practice management course. You will, in addition, be required to complete a forensic accounting course within the first three years of practice.

Third Six

If you are not granted tenancy at the end of your second six, do not despair. There remain a number of routes open to you. Many chambers offer "Third Six" placements for such pupil barristers, by which you will carry out a further six months pupillage at a different chambers with a view to seeking tenancy there at the end. Alternatively, some pupil barristers who do not gain tenancy will choose to go 'in house' to commercial clients or to solicitors firms.

Most chambers will inform you in advance of the completion of your second six whether they intend to offer you tenancy. It is usual (though by no means universal) that you will be informed in time to comply with other sets' Third Six deadlines, but you should ensure that you have researched these deadlines in case you experience any difficulties. Give some early thought as to where you might apply if the tenancy decision does not go your way. Get your applications prepared early and sent out as soon as you receive the decision.

Chapter 16: What to expect: a career at the Bar in perspective.

A typical career?

It is hoped that, having reached this point in the book, you will have realised that there is no such thing as a typical barrister, just as there is no typical set of chambers or even a typical day. The variety of life at the Bar is one of its greatest strengths. Unfortunately for you, that makes it extremely difficult to predict and fully assess.

There is also no such thing as a typical career. As a self-employed individual in a flexible profession, your career is what you make of it. You set the goals, whether your aim is to become a 'Star of the Bar' or simply to enjoy your work whilst maintaining a healthy work/life balance.

The best way of seeing life as a barrister in its various forms is by doing as much work experience as you can. Apply early and apply widely.

Typical features

Nevertheless, there are a number of experiences that will be common to most barristers in the course of their career.

Most begin, as a junior in chambers, doing low value work, or work for clients unable to afford more senior representation. You will be sent off, across the country, for fees barely more than the claim value, or perhaps barely more than the cost of your train ticket. You will have prepared disproportionately for your first hearing: you may have won it, you may have lost, but you will never forget it.

Most will carry out a mixture of written work and court-based advocacy. Some will attend mediations and other out-of-court settlement procedures. The work will gradually increase in value and complexity, and your fees will likewise increase. So too will your confidence, and you will soon feel comfortable discussing the legal procedures or substantive law with your clients and solicitors without having to prepare for hours in advance.

You may also work with those senior to you in chambers, either as a junior to a QC, or as part of a team in a larger or more complex case. You will be carrying out the menial or time-consuming tasks, which would be disproportionate for your leader to undertake, but you will gain good introductions to solicitors and experience in 'better quality' work.

As you develop your own processes and style, you will find that you speed up significantly in the work you are doing and that your abilities in Court 'on your feet' rapidly improve. You will also develop relationships with instructing solicitors, who will give you repeat work.

You may decide it is time for a holiday, and, except for any existing work commitments, will find that you have complete control in marking out in your diary the time you would like to take off. You may decide to take 2 weeks over Christmas, a month over summer, and nobody will stop you. You are self-employed!

You will also decide the working hours you keep, and where you spend them.

There will be many knocks along the way. There will be losses in Court where you feel you should have won, after which you will go over in your head, time and again, what went wrong or what you could have done better. It will be disappointing, but you will learn from it. There will be criticisms from clients or solicitors, some justified, some not, some merely seeking to cover their own backs flowing from their own acts or advice.

You will, not long after you begin, start to feel the stresses and strains; the pressures of being the individual at the end of the chain, representing your client, the only person standing between victory and loss.

You may find that your clerks have accepted too much work on your behalf, or that you have misjudged the time required for work you have accepted, leading to you working some late nights and long weekends. The balance of taking on the right amount of work is a fine and difficult one, which will take many months (if not years) to get right.

Depending on specialism, there may also be more marketing of yourself than you ever expected, whether in the form of seminars and lectures or of food and drink based post-work social activities, usually described as 'networking'. Many barristers excel at marketing themselves in this way; many find it excruciatingly awkward. But, it will pay off and, as you raise your profile, the work will start to flow in.

 These experiences do not stop as your career continues and progresses. You will become better at handling and responding to them, and you will learn to deal with the pressures but, as a self-employed individual, you are always going to be the one at the end of the chain, there to resolve the situation to achieve the best possible outcome for your client. That is both the best and the worst part of the job: you are valuable, your advice and actions influence the steps taken; but the responsibility falls on your shoulders.

Concluding Remarks

A career at the self-employed Bar certainly lends itself to a particular personality type. Independent-minded, self-confident and ambitious individuals can thrive from the freedom available to them.

For those comfortable with the demands and who have the motivation required, it is a highly fulfilling career. You are free to choose your working hours, schedule, holiday and method of working; your oral and written presentational style are likewise yours to decide; you choose what type of work you wish to take on and how you will market yourself.

You are the end of the chain; the legal advisor of last resort. Your opinion matters, and your performance in Court will often be determinative of success or failure for your client. The diversity of work available is second to none, and you will quickly find that you have become knowledgeable about any number of unusual areas of life. Your development and career progression is based on your own merit, and you are free to go as far as your ambition and talent will take you.

But you should go into the profession with your eyes wide open. It is not all meadows and sunshine. It is fiercely competitive and the vast majority of hopefuls never make it. If you do, you will have none of the benefits that come with being someone else's employee. You will have no company pension and no in-work benefits; there is nobody to whom you can delegate when busy; you have no fixed and regular income and may often find yourself with cash-flow difficulties where clients fail to pay on time. As advisor of last resort and the client's representation in Court, the responsibility and pressure on you constantly to perform at your best is high, and stress levels can be severe. Expanding your client base can be reliant on your ability to market yourself, which requires an entirely different skillset. Illness or fatigue are not usually an adequate justification for missing important deadlines which could jeopardise your client's interests. You may be required to work late nights, weekends and during holidays.

You must now ask yourself on which side of the line you fall. Are any of the negatives unacceptable to you? Do the positives make up for them many times over?

Whatever you choose to do, I wish you the very best of luck.

Appendix 1: Sample CVs

Your CV should be tailored to the stage you have reached. By the time you come to apply for pupillage, you will be wanting to cut out some of the qualifications obtained whilst at school in order to make room for your more recent University qualifications.

The first CV set out below comes at an earlier stage in the process (early mini-pupillage stage); and the second CV is written to represent a candidate who has completed the BPTC.

The sample CVs below are for illustrative purposes. They are a guide only. You can include categories of information not set out in the samples if it is information which would improve your application. You should also search for other templates online to get a feel for other ways in which the information can be set out. Ultimately, you should make sure that your CV conveys the image you wish to present of yourself.

LAURA LAWYER

12 Generic Road
Legalton
AB1 2CD

Personal Information

Date of Birth: 12.12.92
Nationality: British.
Tel: 01234 567890
Email: laura.lawyer@gmail.com

Education

Excellent University (2014-2017):

LLB Law

1st Year Papers:

Constitutional	1st	*(145)*
Tort	2:1	*(132)*
Criminal	1st	*(148)*
Civil (Roman)	2:1	*(129)*

Awarded the *Legal Excellence Prize*

2nd Year Papers:

Family	*predicted 1st*
Land	*predicted 2:1*
Contract	*predicted 2:1*
International	*predicted 1st*
Administrative	*predicted 2:1*

Marvellous School, Cranberry (2007-2014)

A-levels:

Maths	– Grade A*	German	– Grade A*
History	– Grade A*	General Studies	– Grade A
Music	– Grade A		

GCSEs:

5 subjects at A* level; 6 subjects at A level.

Awarded Senior History Prize, Senior German Prize and Cranberry Bank Prize for A-Level resu
(2014), and the Sixth Form Scholarship for GCSE results (2012).

Work Experience

Mini-pupillages:
- Easy Court Chambers Lincoln's Inn Fields, London   (25th - 27th June 2014)
- 3 North Square Gray's Inn, London   (23rd June 2014)
- 5 Terrace Buildings Gray's Inn, London   (13th - 14th March 2015)

Marshalling:
- Lord Justice Farrington, Court of Appeal RCJ   (14th April 2014)

Further legal experience:
- Elf Court Chambers Open Day 7 Elf St, London   (3rd December 2013)
- Jason Judge (barrister) 5 Theodore Square Chambers, Leeds   (Three weeks, Summer 2009

Positions of Responsibility

- Treasurer, Greenfield Charity (2010-2014)
- Elected Representative, Excellent University Law Faculty Staff-Student Committee (2014-2015)
- Contributor, Excellent University Alternative Prospectus (20014-)
- Editor, *The BlueCoat*, School Magazine (2012-2014)
- Senior Prefect, Marvellous School (2013-2014); 6th Form Prefect, Marvellous School (2013-2013)

Extra-curricula Activities

Mooting & Debating:
- Excellent University Representative and Winner of the Shrover Exhibition Moot (Nov 2014)
- Excellent University Freshers' Mooting Competition Runner-Up (2014-2015)
- Debating representative for school against others in the region (2012-2014)

Music & Drama:
- Excellent University Operatic Society (*The Marriage of Figaro* – Nov 2014)
- Farnworth Drama Society (*The Tempest, Shakespeare* – Feb 2014)
- Awarded 3 Year Music Scholarship for Performance at Excellent University (Oct 2014)
- 'Tom Cats' Excellent University à cappella choir (2014-)
- Piano, Grade 8 (Winner of various categories in Music Festivals around Cranberryshire)

Sports
- Cranberry Ladies' Rugby Team (2006-8)

Further achievements:
- Leading Law Firm Negotiations Competition, Runner-Up (26th Jan 2015)
- Member of Mensa (2008-)

Voluntary Service:
- Cranberry Hospice, fortnightly volunteering and assisting (2006-2009)
- Barnados Charity Shop Cashier and Stockist (2007-2009)
- Active Citizen Award (2008), awarded by the Cranberry District Council

Referees

Excellent University, Director of Studies
Professor C. Leverclogs
12 Grange Road
Hullby HL14 6GJ
c.lever@excellent.ac.uk

Marvellous School, Form Tutor, 6th Form
Mrs. Dorothy Iligent
Marvellous School,
Country Road,
Cranberry CR5 6AN
d.iligent @school.net

Curriculum Vitae

JEREMY D. JUDGE

81 Cornfield Hill, Huddersfield, HD5 6JL

Tel: 01234 567890 ● Email: Jeremy.Judge@hotmail.com

PERSONAL

Date of Birth:	10.10.1995
Nationality:	British
Languages:	English, French, German

EDUCATION

BKP Law School, Leeds (2015-2016)
BPTC – Outstanding

University of Cambridge, Elliel College (2011-2015)
Law B.A.– 1st Class

University of Pau, France (2013-2014)
Diplôme Universitaire d'Études Juridiques Françaises – 1st Class

Gallston Grammar School, Hudderfield (2004-2011)
A-level – 5 A*s
GCSE – 10 A*s

SCHOLARSHIPS, AWARDS & PRIZES

- Princess Royal Scholarship, 2015 (Inner Temple)
- Advocacy Scholarship, 2015 (BKP Law School, Manchester)
- Villium Prize for Contract Law, 2012 (highest results, University of Cambridge)
- Foundation Scholarship, 2012 (for degree results, Elliel College)
- Senior History and French Prizes, 2011 (A Level Results)
- Ferdinand-Jones Prize, 2011 (overall A-Level results)

POSITIONS OF RESPONSIBILITY

2015 - 16	Advocacy Committee, BKP Law School, Manchester
2012 - 5	Treasurer, Elliel College Law Society
	Elected Representative, Cambridge Law Faculty Staff-Student Committee
2013 -	Contributor, Cambridge University Alternative Prospectus
2009 - 11	Editor, *The WaistCoat*, School Magazine
	Head Boy Team (Senior Prefect), Gallston Grammar School
2009 - 10	6th Form Prefect, Gallston Grammar School

LEGAL WORK EXPERIENCE

Mini-pupillages:

2014	**8 South Square** Gray's Inn, London
	56 Crown Office Row Temple, London
	Great Peace Chambers 475 Stone Buildings, Lincoln's Inn, London
	7 Pump Court Temple, London
	12 New Square Lincoln's Inn, London
	6 Verulam Buildings Gray's Inn, London
	Cogitans Chambers 10 Fleet Street, London
2013	**Toomey Court Chambers** 512 Lincoln's Inn Fields, London
	10 South Square Gray's Inn, London

Marshalling:

2015	HHJ Gareth Winton, Southwark Crown Court
2014	Lady Justice Hubbard, Court of Appeal RCJ

Further legal experience:

2013	RJ Myers Solicitors Vacation Scheme
	Hunter & Hunter LLP Vacation Scheme
2009	Felicity Unwin (barrister) 8 Crimolo Chambers, Leeds

OTHER WORK EXPERIENCE & VOLUNTARY SERVICE

2015	Translator (English-French), Food Aid Relief Fund
2014	English Teacher for French students (aged 16-18), Lycée Camus, Pau
2006 - 10	Scope Charity Shop Cashier and Stockist

PUBLIC SPEAKING & ADVOCACY EXPERIENCE

2016	Outer Temple Advocacy Competition, BKP Law School
2015	Contract Law Speed-Moot, BKP Law School
2014	2 Essex Street Speed-Moot, University of Cambridge
	Elementary Chambers Moot, University of Cambridge
2012	Hunter & Hunter Negotiations Competition, Runner-Up
2008 – 11	Regional Debating Representative for school

INTERESTS

I am particularly interested in music and drama:

2016	Inner Temple Drama Society, *Fidget Fingers! The Barrister who always typed.*
2012 - 15	Cambridge University Gilbert & Sullivan Society (*various*)
2012	Elliel College Chapel Choir, Bass
2011 - 14	'Tabbies' Cambridge University à cappella choir
2006 - 11	Piano (Grade 8), Trumpet (Grade 7) & Winner in Music Festivals around Yorkshire

REFEREES

Director of Studies
Professor Christine Leverlogs
Elliel College
Cambridge
CB2 3DE
c.leverclogs@cam.ac.uk

Dean of College & Supervisor of
International Law and Conflict of Laws
Dr. Bernard Rainybox
Elliel College
Cambridge
CB2 3DE
b.rainybox@cam.ac.uk

Index

A

acting, 80, 122
advocacy, 103, 108
A-Levels, 61
appearance, 109
applications, 28, 44, 55, 58, 61, 65, 74, 94, 100, 101, 102, 113, 128
assessment criteria, 103
associations, 23, 51
atmosphere, 38, 73, 97, 98
awards, 44, 66, 103, 112

B

Bar Course Aptitude Test, 64
Bar Mutual Indemnity Fund, 85
Bar Professional Training Course, 43, 54, 63
BCAT, 64
Benchers, 43
BPTC, 43, 44, 47, 52, 54, 63, 64, 65, 66, 67, 82, 135
Briggs Review, 122

C

cab rank rule, 24

D

E

F

favouritism, 2
fees, 22, 36, 38, 40, 67, 92, 93, 130
foundation subjects, 53, 58, 62, 89
Free Representation Unit, 82
FRU, 82
funding, 43, 44, 47, 66

G

Gateway, 101, 102
GCSE, 61
GDL, 26, 30, 43, 44, 51, 52, 53, 54, 55, 58, 60, 65, 74, 85, 90
Graduate Diploma in Law, 26, 43, 53, 58
Gray's Inn, 42, 83

H

holiday, 38, 131, 132

I

income, 92
independence, 82, 123, 126
Inn, 44, 45, 47, 51, 65, 76, 110, 124, 127
Inner Temple, 42
Inns, 42, 43, 44, 45, 46, 47, 50, 52, 65, 66, 68, 71, 76, 91, 98
Inns of Court, 42, 43, 50, 52, 65, 66, 68, 76, 91, 98
instructions, 22, 23
integrity, 81, 82, 105
Interest in the Law, 8
Inter-personal Skills, 80
interview, 3, 44, 74, 77, 101, 102, 103, 105, 106, 107, 109, 110, 112, 115, 122, 123

J

Jackson Review, 120
judgments, 91, 94, 99

L

Law Commission, 122
Law Degree, 54
law fairs, 83
legal advice centres, 82
legislation, 2, 6, 8, 9, 10, 14, 16, 115, 120
libraries, 46, 91, 94
Limitation Act 1980, 9
limitation periods, 9
Lincoln's Inn, 42
LNAT, 57
Location, 96

M

marketing, 39, 75, 98, 132
marshalling, 70, 75, 76
mentor, 45, 110
meritocratic, 3
Middle Temple, 42
mini-pupillage, 51, 62, 70, 71, 72, 73, 74, 109, 110, 113, 135
mock interview, 110
Mode of Work, 25
modules, 54, 62, 90, 94
mooting, 57, 79, 103

N

National Admissions Test for Law, 57
negligence, 9, 15, 32, 60
nuisance, 14, 15, 16

O

open days, 47, 51, 59, 66
Outreach, 46

P

Paralegals, 30
Parliament, 8, 9, 14, 16, 120
pressures, 91, 131, 132
Pro Bono, 82
provinces, 96
public speaking, 79, 80, 103, 112
publications, 81
Pupil Supervisors, 124
pupillage fairs, 83, 98
Pupillage Gateway, 101, 113

Q

QASA, 122
Qualifying Law Degree, 53
qualifying sessions, 43, 44, 52
Quality Assurance Scheme for Advocates, 122
Queen's Counsel, 25

R

rankings agencies, 86
referees, 105
reference, 64, 106, 115, 116, 117, 122
reputation, 33, 34, 39, 40, 56, 81, 98, 100, 105
residential weekends, 45, 52
risk, 3, 67
role, 6, 20, 24, 28, 30, 33, 43, 82, 98
    Barristers, 6, 20
    Chartered Legal Executives, 20, 30

Printed in Great Britain
by Amazon